MW01096398

The Limerick, *Restored*

A Seminal Revitalization of the Literary Tradition

THE POXY BROTHERS

If you enjoy this book:

Please support boundary-pushing art and free expression with a review or rating on Amazon, Google, Goodreads, or another platform! We thank you from the bottom of our hearts for your support.

A REMARK ON THE LIKELIHOOD OF FRIVOLOUS USES FOR THIS BOOK

For those seeking a cheap laugh, I strongly implore you to look elsewhere. *The Limerick, Restored* is a work of literature, not a gag gift for your sophomoric uncle. It is far too advanced to be enjoyed by philistines.

However:

For serious intellectuals, devoted vocabularians, and literary historians seeking a linguistic feast to challenge and delight them, this volume is the perfect solution.

Yours Truly,

Gulliver Einhorn, Esq.
Personal Representative of the Poxy Brothers

CONTENTS

FOREWORD

Congratulations! By purchasing this volume, you are participating in the restoration of a culture from the brink of total collapse. Please, allow me to explain.

The limerick is a type of folk poem with its origins in the early 18th-century Anglo world. Often hilariously erotic, limericks constitute an essential literary category in the canon of English poetry. But with the 21st-century rise of political correctness, this great tradition has been reduced to a pathetic, shriveled version of its former self. No truly brilliant collection of originals has been seen in decades, and the anthologies are gathering dust.

With nowhere else to turn, the literati of today are relegated to digging up old copies of out-of-print classics to satisfy their lust for the vile hilarity, delightful vocabulary, and singsong rhythm of this vital poetic form. This decline is a great loss for the art and literature world, and a tragedy for our language at large.

Once a pillar of literary humor, the decline of the X-rated limerick represents the decline of civilization itself; a symbol of our cultural descent into a world of bland, dystopic sterility and aimless outrage.

It's time that this wrong was righted. To that end, please enjoy this book of over 1,000 original limericks for a fresh generation; a collection of delightfully disgusting poems replete with modern references for the new century's readers. Old students of the limerick desperate for new material will be delighted to find it here, and those still uninitiated into this important English tradition can now discover it in earnest.

Your participation in this cultural revitalization is nothing short of historic.

Onward!

Gulliver Einhorn, Esq.
Personal Representative of the Poxy Brothers

SECTION I:
Technology & Internet Porn

The Limerick,
Restored

The Alexa we put in our home
Listens whenever we bone…
It hears lots of slaps
When we fuck and we fap,
While Bezos gets off to the groans

Dreadfully desensitized
By the porn that once dazzled his eyes,
The addict, depraved,
Took to fucking on graves,
And acts too wrong to describe

I bought a new phone with two screens,
To watch porno with double the teens…
It doubled my load,
But also bestowed
An obsession with cheerleader scenes

SECTION I:
Technology & Internet Porn

When Zuckerberg strokes out some splooge,
The data is presently used
To serve ads to the stuff
That gets made in his nuts,
As their privacy's promptly abused

A millennial, wracked by ennui,
Was driven to drink her own pee…
When she streamed it online,
'Twas delighted to find,
They tipped her a fortune in fees

A wealthy, coke-addled homo
Suffered from Instagram FOMO
Seeking more likes,
Posted pics of young dykes, and
Deep-dicking his house majordomo

The Limerick,
Restored

A live streamer discovered, quite roundly,
She'd increase her viewers profoundly
By becoming more vile
'Till, covered in bile,
She was driven to act quite unsoundly

A smut star, retired, was scorned
From any profession but porn…
She came back to do cams,
Fucked herself with a lamp,
And like that, her career was reborn

On nearly all of the Chans,
Legions of anime fans
Alone in their rooms,
Whack off to cartoons
Of lolis with mountainous cans

4

SECTION I:
Technology & Internet Porn

A dark obsession with breeding
Betrayed a man who was cheating:
Soon the ole' lout
Was duly found out
When his kids found the brags he was tweeting

A perfectly typical tot
Became a promiscuous thot…
For the porn in her phone,
Of teens being boned,
Had her touching her wet little spot

A spam ad came through my email
Vowing triumph where others have failed:
It swears I'll be thicker
For when I deep dick 'er
By drinking the slime of a snail

The Limerick,
Restored

Nasty images hidden in Disney
Have me jerking off in a tizzy
From Elsa to Belle,
I live very well,
But my screens have all become jizzy

When too much weird porn left him numb,
Stroking off was no longer fun…
So his tastes became darker:
Like carnival barkers
Bathing the freaks in their cum

Immersed in porn VR goggles,
He watched so much smut that it boggles
The mind to imagine
His raw one-eyed dragon,
With blood and scabs on the nozzle

His silhouette basked in the glow
From what his monitor showed:
Clearly he's jerking
For hours, and lurking
On gifs of tits bouncing slow-mo

A hottie this fiend met on Tinder
Was distressed when he tackled and skinned her
He put her skin on,
Stacked some wood in the lawn,
And burnt that bod a cinder

A curvy, affection-starved lass
Was the envy of none in her class…
But her Instagram soared
When she dressed like a whore,
And showed off the size of her ass

The Limerick,
Restored

My buddy, he programmed an app,
Where you put your phone onto your lap…
It vibrates so fast
It'll tickle your ass,
And drain all your masculine sap

A filthy limerick on Reddit
Offended me when I said it:
The poster, a crook
Stole it straight from this book,
Without even giving me credit

An online relationship fizzled
For in person, it just lacked the sizzle…
Instead of a shower
Of cream from his tower,
'Twas more of an ooze and a drizzle

SECTION I:
Technology & Internet Porn

After posting her cumshot online,
The commenters sent her a sign
That she could go pro,
And do nothing but blow,
And get paid to get blasted with slime

A boyfriend, feeling unsexed,
Mentioned it to his gal in a text…
From convo banal
To the slapping of balls;
Stuffed 'till he cums on her chest

A girl DM'd me on Twitter,
Inviting me into her shitter…
But with @analslut8,
The sex wasn't great:
'Twas so gaping, my dick didn't fit'er

The Limerick,
Restored

A more common use than I supposed
For a young lady's old clothes
Is to sell them online,
For the odor of 'gine
Is quite a thrill to the nose

A mom put her child in theatre,
And soon, TV watchers revered her...
But her biggest fans
In kid pageant land
Deplorably, wanted to spear her

The algos found your family vids
Of that Florida trip with the kids...
But YouTube is serving
The clips to guys perving
For kids that'd stick to their ribs

A toddler watching TV
Was affected by what she could see:
The influence working
Of sexual twerking,
Learned by a girl of three

Through the study of smut, I have learned
That most gals like a fucking so firm
That it rocks their insides
When I hop on and ride,
Slamming my coital worm

Your lover, long-gone on a plane,
Will still pleasure your little membrane…
Teledildonics
Will boggle our bonnets;
We're fucking with only our brains

The Limerick,
Restored

A man swore off women of flesh,
For silicone babes he liked best…
He constantly sinned,
But instead of skin,
'Twas rubbery pussy and breasts

Thank goodness they banned all the vaping,
For many-a teen was left gaping…
Curiosity reigns,
For teens gone insane
With objects their pussies are taking

A soulless doll, with AI,
Can now look you right in your eyes,
Say, "I love you so much,
I long for your touch,
I live for the thing in your thighs."

The phones that we keep in our pockets—
The sperm that we make, they will block it
So much radiation,
In aggregation,
Is roasting the fruit of our rockets

To my love, I finally confessed,
But then was severely depressed...
When she left me on Read,
I wished I was dead:
I shouldn't have chosen to text

After a marathon of pussy and tit shit,
I checked the results on my FitBit:
28,000 steps
(But it was just sex),
Slamming my dong in a dick slit

The Limerick,
Restored

In footage unique and bizarre,
A singer played on his guitar…
But instead of a pick,
He played with his dick,
Which made him an Internet star

The inescapable truth
Is that we have corrupted the youth…
I blame the screens
For promoting to teens
The vulgar, depraved, and uncouth

An app that some women detest
Makes use of your phone's GPS
So you can track down,
At bars in your town,
The women with walloping breasts

SECTION I:
Technology & Internet Porn

Our nightmare, foreseen by Orwell,
Is a dreadful sexual hell…
For when we're being nailed,
We're being surveilled
By a staff of depraved personnel

Have you ever been fucked by a robot?
Their cyber-pussies are so hot…
They use algorithms
To draw out your jism,
Extracting your masculine man-snot

When you spend your ripest young days
In a cock-numbing, porn-addled haze,
All of that porn
Will leave you forlorn,
And shriveled from what it portrays

The Limerick,
Restored

My sex robot beeped into gear,
But a virus installed made it queer:
　　Due to the glitches,
　　Now I need stitches
From what it has done to my rear

On Bumble I made a sweet match,
Who swiftly gave me her snatch…
　　While I was piping,
　　I also was swiping,
And now she thinks that I am trash

Pics of which I wasn't proud,
And I thought were safe on the cloud,
　　Were hacked, and revealed
　　My masculine eel
To international crowds

SECTION I:
Technology & Internet Porn

I was banned from a platform called TikTok
For posting a vid of my big cock…
The app is for prudes—
They don't allow nudes,
Which came to me as a big shock

There you are, on your Kindle,
Reading and feeling the tingle,
Getting wet off of rhymes
About seminal slime…
No wonder you are still single

She logged onto her phone and computer
To browse for a suitable suitor…
But her gentleman caller
Just wanted to maul her,
And pummel her hot little cooter

The Limerick,
Restored

I fucked her so hard in her Lexus,
It jabbed hard into her solar plexus...
She wanted it hard
In the back of her car,
But there's risks to the rough kinds of sexes

In the back of a Tesla, self-driving,
A cock and a cunt were colliding...
They fucked extra hard
When the brakes of the car
Were seized by a hacker in hiding

Celebrity sexts have been hacked
So the creepers on 4Chan can fap...
Private pics that they cherished
Have left them embarrassed,
While creeps do a victory lap

SECTION I:
Technology & Internet Porn

I downloaded the messenger, Kik,
To send girls a pic of my dick…
It inspired their lust,
So one helped me bust,
By lending a suck and a lick

Lots of Instagram thots
Are obsessed with stair climbers and squats:
The biggest ass gets the likes
From guys who wanna spike
An ass that's incredibly hot

A device for pudendal vibration
Encouraged her pussy's hydration:
A handheld pleasure-giver
Has brought forth a river,
Along with orgasmic gyration

The Limerick,
Restored

I thought I'd slide into her mentions,
Hoping to snag her attention...
I messaged my cock,
And then I was blocked,
But had only the sweetest intentions

At the Audubon, early one morn,
I recognized someone from porn...
The web's biggest squirter
Is also a birder
With habits quite nasty, I warn

For years, the pleasure I sought
I later found out could be bought:
A pussy so grand
In the palm of my hand,
In the form of a silicone twat

SECTION I:
Technology & Internet Porn

Remember when porn was still naughty,
'Cause to catch a glimpse of a body,
You snuck to your dad's
To dig up his mags,
And stroke out a glob of your snotty?

I'm a Vlogging content creator…
In other words, an auto-fellator:
My fans and my minions
Love my opinions;
I'm certain they couldn't be greater

I landed a freelancing gig
That paid me in flesh, you dig?
I'd commit some new code,
Then submit a hot load
Out of my quivering twig

The Limerick,
Restored

A hacker took over my Ring
To watch me do prurient things
But he left with a scoff when
I stopped whacking off,
Found the Lord, and confessed to my sins

I saw that my crush had a Pinterest,
So I pinned up some pictures of interest…
Me holding my dick;
A veiny and thick
Spectacle for her to witness

A student, in need of some cash,
Might make a decision too rash…
Your porno endeavor
Is out there forever;
I'll find it online in a flash

SECTION I:
Technology & Internet Porn

I'm a little bit miffed
By the driver of this morning's Lyft:
During the ride,
He locked me inside,
And forced me to suck on his stiff

This bitcoiner, name of Neeraj,
His coins were reduced to mirage:
Left his seed at Penn Station,
During masturbation,
And hung himself in his garage

I typed in just one dirty question,
And now receive ads every session:
"Grow your dick seven inches!"
"Local nipples need pinches!" —
The web thinks I have an obsession

The Limerick,
Restored

My mom caught me looking at hooters
On all of the family computers…
But now, to get hard,
My phone is the card
For sneaking a peep at some nuders

I make thousands working from home
By filming the girls I bone…
They do not know
That each fuck and blow
Will play on one million phones

Humanity's oldest profession
Has become quite an obsession:
Each night online,
I pay what I find,
To help me complete my transgression

SECTION I:
Technology & Internet Porn

I hang my head, for I mourn
The death of my masculine horn:
I rubbed it so hard
That it's deadened and scarred
From decades of jerking to porn

She drank herself into a stupor,
And tumbled into her Uber
She paid her driver
With more than a fiver,
Sucking his vascular goober

My seminal flow, so unending,
Has made me a web topic trending:
Men want to know
My secret to blow
The gallons of cum I'm expending

The Limerick,
Restored

I finally moved into the city, and
Used an app to find dates, young and pretty
In lands much more rural,
It's hard to find girls
To let you come tickle their kitty

After my penis has grown,
It shoots out the seminal foam…
Especially when
I'm chatting with Jen,
Sexting her over the phone

SECTION II:
Literature, Pop Culture, & The Arts

The Limerick,
Restored

A belligerent chef, name of Gordon
Screamed at his trainee like a warden…
But the gal had a fetish,
So feeling coquettish,
She attempted to whack off his organ

A billionaire, name of Buffett,
Despite being old, loved to stuff it
Into every last hole
He could find for his pole,
Including a silicone puppet

Despite being burned in a fire,
A gal was still hot with desire…
Once a full ten,
Now she only gets men
Who look like they came from the Shire

A new movie starring The Rock,
Like peanuts hung under a glock,
Showed what was shrunken
From roids he was pumpin'
When they revealed his cock

Her Brobdingnagian tits
Sent men into sexual fits…
But things became stranger
When, nude in the manger,
They spotted her seven-inch clit

The Wonderland witnessed by Alice
Was nightmarish, after a chalice
Of wine from the Queen
Knocked out the pre-teen,
And guards took their turns at the palace

The Limerick,
Restored

The Johnson of A-lister Dwayne
Left many-a pussy in pain:
Once it got growin',
This beefy Samoan
Had penis as big as a train

An orgy at Burning Man festival
Turned out to be bad and detestable:
'Twas so much cum and lube
That the dome came unglued,
And now they have dust on their genitals

I once knew a man from Nantucket
Who kept all his cum in a bucket…
A slave did submit
When it dumped on her slit,
And then he was ready to fuck it

A mobster, completely oogatz,
Got whacked on the big boss' yacht
Said "Ya wife's my goomar"—
Then he jumped on the bar—
"And ya daughtah, I fingered her twat!"

An actor once great, Cuba Gooding
Found himself on precarious footing:
For reports all accounted
That women he mounted,
Forcing his chocolatey pudding

Afflictions aside, Helen Keller—
Her nose and her pussy were stellar
She'd be sniffing around
To find cocks in her town,
Using her sexual smeller

The Limerick,
Restored

El narcotraficante, El Chapo
No tiene un cuerpo muy guapo…
Todas las putas
Sobre sus rutas
Toman su pene, muy flaco

A movie where dozens are slaughtered
Might be one where you take your daughter…
But with lesbian sex
It will be rated X,
And would make you a very bad father

A man with a wiener, grotesque
Got hard at a show of burlesque
It burst through his fly,
To horrified eyes,
Looking quite Dr. Seuss-esque

In a conflict between Luke and Han,
They decided to leave all their bygones…
Luke relinquished his kin
So that Solo could sin,
And give Chewie a turn for the pile-on

There once was a passionate Brony
And during his testimony,
He told the judge
That he wanted some fudge,
And that's why he bum-fucked the pony

A goomba thought I was a fool
For failing my way out of school
At our tutoring session,
He taught me a lesson,
And gave me his hard gabagool

The Limerick,
Restored

Rapunzel, so I am told,
Just liked for her hair to be pulled…
Her ploy was a prank
To get him to yank;
A kink spiraled out of control

The little known fact of Camus
Was an existential obsession with poo:
Feeling no danger,
Crouched under a Stranger,
Sliding with glee in their stew

Poetry, see, is too boring
Without all these tales of whoring…
That's why I prefer
Something sexy occur,
For laughing and hooting and roaring

In a match of professional wrestling,
Sweaty man-bodies were nestling…
On came defeat
When the champ touched his meat,
Working the cream from his vessel-thing

Poetry, always so serious,
Is dark, and sad, and mysterious
I'd rather rest
Doing what I do best:
Jerk off until I'm delirious

Hickory, dickory, dock
The mouth, it sucks a cock
The clock strikes one,
Out comes the cum:
Hickory, dickory, dock

The Limerick,
Restored

I awoke, and my vision was blurry,
And I found I'd been drugged by a Furry
In his dog suit, he barked
While he humped in the dark,
And filled me with animal slurry

Old Hemingway, down in the bush,
Lusted after his rough ranger's tush
"When I give him Campari
On every safari,
He swallows my heavenly mush."

Just weeks after I achieved fame,
I was drugged and abused by a dame...
That piece of whore trash
Left me with a rash,
Along with unbearable shame

In pursuit of her labia menorah,
He put on his finest fedora
But the cringey neckbeard,
Just as he'd always feared,
Was rejected again by señora

Aboard an assignment quite cushy,
Captain Nemo became rather pushy
Rock-hard and horny
During his journey,
20,000 leagues under a pussy

When you're fucking, be sure to play music
To fit the sex style you're choosing:
Some Bach if it's passionate,
But if you're just mashin' it,
Metal goes well with a bruising

The Limerick,
Restored

When she sings us her musical tune,
We know we'll be hard very soon…
Her sexual vocals
Arouse all the locals,
Stroking alone in our rooms

The trope, as a reader might guess,
When the knight is a Judy or Bess,
Is the person she'll save
From the castle or cave
Is a Daniel in distress

Speaking of Ricky Gervais,
I'd certainly like him to lay us
But the thing he must see
Is this ass isn't free:
To get it, he'll first have to pay us

The most hideous thing about Grendel
Was no doubt his organ, pudendal
He captured a lady
And fucked her like crazy,
With nary a knight to defend 'er

When the rock star bedded the groupie,
Some drugs had left her quite loopy…
To make matters worse,
His size was a curse,
Leaving her drooping and soupy

Skitching up tart goober globbus,
Canoodling moistman up slobbus,
Slurp-addled suck big,
Gulp tiddlywig,
Blob globby in twerpington throbbus

The Limerick,
Restored

You say that my poems offend you?
Here is a tip I will lend you:
Go cry somewhere else,
Reflect on yourself,
And maybe I'll even befriend you

This hot TV dyke, Rachel Maddow
Is a lesbo I wish I could shag now
This Russiagate nerder
Will soon be a squirter;
The gay pussy I'm gonna grab now

The pundit, Stefan Molyneux
Admires a powerful goo…
He loves the causation
Of fertilization,
After a martial screw

For the actor, Tobey Maguire,
Things had become rather dire…
He was tied to a beam
For a really tough scene
Involving a torch and some wire

Gwyneth Paltrow met up in New York,
Eager for someone to pork…
We got to third base,
With my Goop on her face,
Shot from the tip of my cork

Regarding the ole' Family Addams,
Morticia's a hot little madam:
Her pale white skin
Tempts me to sin,
And her titties—I wanna gram em'

The Limerick,
Restored

Like a thing from a story by Borges,
My mythical babe is so gorgeous:
She has wings like a bat,
And her bootie is fat,
So I'm fucking her vaginal fortress

A is for Anna, a slut
B's for her tight little Butt
C is for Cum,
The D's where it's from,
And E for Ejection of nut

There once was a butt-loving rapper
Who always dressed fancy and dapper...
This impressed who he liked,
And wanted to spike,
Stuffing their fabulous crapper

Regarding the babe, Agent Scully,
I wanted to fuck her so fully…
But that bastard Duchovny
Was in line above me,
And now her vagina's been sullied

Chomsky, a famous free thinker,
Loved to fuck gals in their stinker…
Thinking outside the box
Meant more holes for his cock,
And new ways to sexually tinker

When in comes the rap star Tyrese,
Better get out the lube and the grease:
He's furious n' fast
When he cums up your ass
With his vascular, masculine piece

The Limerick,
Restored

The actor, Sylvester Stallone,
Can really cause em' to moan…
The big star of Rocky
Can be pretty cocky
When he is thrusting his bone

Lustful ole' Coco Joe
Used to love hookers and blow…
Now with his voice so hoarse,
He has stories, of course,
To tell on the Joe Rogan show

When Tarzan fucked hot little Jane,
His nuts quite in need of a drain,
The boy of the jungle
Was rough with the tumble,
Leaving her pussy in pain

I was strolling the Yellow Brick Road
Straight toward the Wizard's abode
'Cause me and a munchkin
Were double-dick dunkin',
To give little Dorothy a load

The angle, rhythm, and timing
Is what gets an orgasm climbing…
So I'm using my pelvis,
Rockin' like Elvis,
To give her one helluva sliming

Tarantino is feeling the heat
From his sexual fixation with feet:
One toe that he sucked
Was too young to be fucked;
Now Quentin is off of the street

The Limerick,
Restored

I heard that the actor Mark Hamill
Gives his saber to all kinds of mammals:
He once fucked a sheep
Named Little Bo Peep,
And another time, mounted a camel

A mousey young gal, name of Minnie,
Took a look at my cock and said, "Gimme!"
So she sucked on my Mickey,
'Till out came the sticky,
Blowing all over her chinnie

Given a *this* and a *that,*
I'd choose *that,* as a matter of fact…
I like *that* a lot,
When *that* is a twat:
A vagina, to be exact

A real dumb fella named Gump
Wasn't smart, but boy could he hump…
And Lieutenant Dan
Will lend him a hand,
And help him find holes for his junk

When Peter Pan anal-fucked Tinkerbell,
He quickly detected a stink n' smell…
But her stinky farter
Only got Peter harder—
The boy, turned out, had a kink as well

Deep in the depths of the sewer,
Ole' Donatello will do 'er:
Using a Sybian,
This teenage reptilian
Will make April cum, and then goo 'er

The Limerick,
Restored

The secret of Winnie the Pooh
Is shocking, but totally true:
Christopher Robin
Was constantly throbbin',
And fucked Winnie full of his goo

Whenever I'd watch Game of Thrones,
I'd just wait for a scene where they'd bone…
When those sweet titties showed,
I'd stroke out a load,
And let out a satisfied groan

In my dream, Scarlett Johanssen
Is topless in panties, and dancing…
Next up comes the suck!
What magnificent luck
That Scarlett and I are romancing

On the top floor of ole' Nakatomi,
John McClane said, "You can blow me."
I said, "Yippie-kay-yay,
Didn't know you were gay,"
Then I sucked on his sweet pepperoni

Mrs. Butterworth, plump and so ripe,
Loved when I gave her my pipe…
Then came my syrup,
And she was so full-up,
Her pussy required a wipe

The star of the ice known as Gretzky
Ran into a problem quite pesky:
The flying black puck
Slammed into his nuts,
And blew away both of his testes

The Limerick,
Restored

A young wizard teen cast a pox
On his rival's formidable cock
Harry's was hairy,
But Draco's was scary:
Hermoine was knocked from her socks

The problem with stars like the Biebers
Is what they can do to young beavers:
Too young to be wet,
It's distressing (at best)
To see them in sexual fevers

Too much pop and molasses
Is known to enlarge women's asses…
But it's great news for some,
Who have tastes like R. Crumb,
Who likes his posteriors massive

In fitness, yoga, and dance,
The gals have to wear stretchy pants:
"Hey babe, Namaste,
Your ass blows me away.
Could I get your number, perchance?"

With the orgasms that she is faking,
An Oscar might be in the making:
She shakes and she shudders,
"G-god yes!" she stutters,
Her pussy dilated and gaping

When I get the ole' writer's block,
And my mind feels clamped in a lock,
My quill begins growing,
And ideas flowing,
The moment I write about cock

The Limerick,
Restored

A sex scene, up on the stage,
Filled ticket-holders with rage:
Defiling the theatre,
She moaned as he speared her,
Acting quite fully engaged

When I watch her reporting the weather,
It rustles my penile tether…
A high-pressure system
Takes hold in my piston,
For storms in my region down nether

I once fucked a kinky songwriter,
Whose pussy just couldn't be tighter
When I tossed her salad,
She'd sing me a ballad,
Squealing whenever I'd bite her

An incel who studied the blade
Was desperate to finally get laid…
So when his crush Shoshanna
Shrugged off his katana,
He forced his way into her glade

My fans, they are really disgusting,
Stroking and sucking and busting,
Reading these tales
Of gals getting nailed,
And men with their animal thrusting

While researching this book as a writer,
I found pussies tighter and tighter…
I fucked every one,
(For work, not for fun),
And pumped them all full of my cider

The Limerick,
Restored

Time to head out with the squad,
To the club to find Jenny some rod…
She's horny and single,
And feeling the tingle,
But has quite a hideous bod

My techniques are rather particular
For crafting a poem testicular:
I cum a few times,
Then whip up some rhymes,
Rubbing my organ orbicular

I'm fucking a fat opera singer
Who I wish was a little bit thinner…
But her vocalization
Creates a pulsation
That orally, makes her a winner

On a date with an arable breeder,
We sat in the back of the theatre
When the first act was up,
She gave me a suck,
And then I decided to seed her

With weather gloomy and gray,
You can go catch a cheap matinée…
You can sit in the back,
Get your penis unpacked,
And rub if the film is risqué

I once knew a chap named Orlando
He was hung, but wasn't quite Brando
On the day of his birth,
He wished for more girth,
Burst his undies, and now goes commando

SECTION III:
Bestiality, Family Life, & Holidays

The Limerick,
Restored

She happened to notice her mastiff
Carried a cock rather massive
She quickly bent over,
Eager for rover,
But poochie was rather impassive

I heard of an unlucky angler
Who frustrated, dipped in his dangler
Well a big bass latched on,
And shook it so strong,
That now, they call him The Mangler

Saint Nick's lascivious plan
Was to peep all the sex in the land…
Making his rounds,
Wanking off in the towns,
Ho-ho-hoing his dick in his hand

I was shocked to see, down at the bog,
My sister was humping a log…
But shocked even more
Walking back through my door
To find grandma rimming the dog

The unsettling case of a nanna
Who fucked herself with bananas
Horrified her whole family,
Who banished the granny,
To die in a barren savannah

When a dad heard his daughter reviled,
He moved to protect the young child
The catcalling pedo
Soon was quite dead-o,
Broken and heaped in a pile

The Limerick,
Restored

Awry went a family safari
And boy, the park ranger was sorry:
The family was twisted,
Seeking animal fistin',
And acts that involved calamari

A cheating husband was caught
When the pet parrot he bought
Repeated at Christmas
The words of his mistress:
"Please darling, pummel my twat!"

A man on his sweet honeymoon
Knew that he'd be divorced soon:
With passionate stuffing,
Still, he felt nothing,
So vast was the size of her poon

SECTION III:
Bestiality, Family Life, & Holidays

He stumbled home late from the pub
Hoping he might get a rub…
But home around three,
A well-hung amputee
Was fucking his wife with the stub

A man of particular ilk
Was obsessed with drinking fresh milk…
But it wasn't bovine—
His wife a goldmine,
Udders softer than silk

In a world gone sick and depraved,
Where it's fetish and fucking we crave,
The final taboo
(It's strange, but it's true)
Is to marry, have kids, and behave

The Limerick,
Restored

At an unfortunate kid's show-and-tell
The teacher detected a smell:
Some kid brought used rubbers
From his mom, a night clubber,
Filled up with seminal gel

On an Icelandic glacier, they toured
And a man used his masculine sword
Fucking his wife's caboose
Shook a chunk of ice loose,
And both fell into a fjord

My father fired the maid,
But I sure wish she could stay…
Tucking me in,
My balls on her chin;
Semen for spit was our trade

SECTION III:
Bestiality, Family Life, & Holidays

Mrs. Claus was feeling quite horny
With Santa away on his journey…
So she summoned some elves,
Made them jerk off themselves,
Enraging the Claus's attorney

Under the lit Christmas tree,
The only gift that I need
Is the mouth of a broad
To stuff with my rod,
And fill with my wintry seed

There once was a crisis, ovarian
That arose from a section, caesarean:
The surgeon, he slipped,
Cut the poor kid to shit,
And now he looks like a barbarian

The Limerick,
Restored

On a rather regrettable Seder,
My embarrassment couldn't be greater...
I was caught with my shank
In my hands as I wanked,
And now I'm a known masturbator

On the lap of ole' jolly Saint Nick
Sat a nubile, busty and thick...
His small red-nosed helper
Grew as he felt her
Grinding her ass on his dick

Rudolph has a red nose
And when he gets horny, it grows...
With one look at Vixen,
Rudolph and Blitzen
Team up to fuck her as bros

My cousin and I are so close,
We hang out without wearing clothes…
Sure, after some drinks
I might tickle her stink,
But it's fine 'long as nobody knows

For reasons evading her mind,
Her hubby's libido declined
But she'd get him hard
If she played her last card:
Poblanos shoved up his behind

Once done on a farm with your chores,
Working out can be such a bore…
But intercourse
On the back of a horse
Is a great way to strengthen the core

The Limerick,
Restored

They're old, decayed, and retired,
But their sex life is fully on fire:
His wrinkly old dingle
Was deep in her pringle
Right up until when they expired

A peeper, crouched in the trees,
A boner between both his knees,
Is using his lookers
To spy on some hookers,
Despite being father to three

When it came to most any test,
On pregnancy tests she scored best…
On kid forty-nine,
She drew the line,
Feeling so weary and stretched

As she watched the dashing old potter,
His fingers just couldn't be hotter…
She was wet at the way
His hands worked the clay—
The problem was, she was his daughter

At the unfaithful lad's holy wedding,
In walked the whore he'd been bedding…
He left with the side chick,
Eager to ride dick,
Ready for sucking and spreading

A horrible, horned Christmas demon
Has come for the naughty this season:
Krampus is here,
But you've nothing to fear—
All he wants is a taste of your semen

The Limerick,
Restored

"Well, since I bring home the bacon,
It's sandwiches that you'll be making."
But the wifey just grinned,
Stomped the chauvinist's shins,
And left him there crumpled and shaken

I found out that I was the father
But anyway, couldn't be bothered…
'Till my kids came and found me,
Beat me, and drowned me:
Justice from sons and from daughters

To practice the art of good fucking,
Just find any gal that needs stuffing…
Sure, it's taboo,
But your sister will do,
And I'm sure that her puss could use puffing

One Christmas, we got kinda boozy,
And fucked in the hotel Jacuzzi…
I felt a bit guilty,
For we got it filthy,
Ruined with wads of my sploogie

The photos of what I had missed
Were given to me on a disc:
After they wed,
And clothes had been shed,
The bride gave a groomsman The Fist

For New Year's, my somber reflection
Resulted in quite the erection:
Thought of all the year's ladies,
Hotter than hades,
I pumped in most every direction

The Limerick,
Restored

I developed a volcanic aversion
While on a Hawaiian excursion…
The volcano blew,
And my father did too,
Revealing a hidden perversion

When Grampa sits down on the porch,
The kids will all chortle and snort:
He'd sit at an angle,
Revealing the dangle,
His nuts hanging out of his shorts

I once had an uncle named Merv,
Who was quite the incurable perv…
We drew the line
As a family, the time
We noticed holes in the hors d'oeuvres

SECTION III:
Bestiality, Family Life, & Holidays

I once had a golden retriever
Who fell into sexual fevers…
His doggie red rocket,
Seeking a pocket,
Knew I would be a receiver

While treating a dog in a rut,
A trainer got close to the mutt
But it only learned "come,"
Mounting her bum,
And ramming its cock in her butt

A father felt awful malaise,
And hoped it was only a phase
When he learned that his son's
Idea of fun
Was slurping his own mayonnaise

The Limerick,
Restored

A young lad's attraction to reptiles
Caused many problems, erectile:
At the dino museum,
His teacher did see him
Squirting a primal projectile

In this case, the matrimony
Is vile, wrong, and unholy:
No little kid
Should marry the squid
Meant for that night's ravioli

After events quite traumatic,
My daughter became quite erratic:
Fucking film canisters,
Humping the banisters,
Hours spent up in the attic

SECTION III:
Bestiality, Family Life, & Holidays

It's impossible, see, to have kids,
Without the injection of jizz
It's a matter of flesh,
Of bodies enmeshed,
And that's just the way that it is

When a cock and a pussy are joined,
It awakens the fruit of the loins
But deliver the gravy,
And you'll make a baby
After the grinding of groins

The butcher's daughter in Keat
Is fond of fresh organ meat
In addition to food,
She'll throat any dude
With a package that's handsome and neat

The Limerick,
Restored

With my potency rapidly fading,
I'm wracked by the process of aging…
My once-rigid cock
Hangs limp like a sock;
My boners are no longer raging

Swapping your hot little wife
Will cure all your marital strife:
The pleasure you're bringing
From all of your swinging
Brings spice to your sexual life

On the glorious night of my wedding,
My new wifey's legs were a-spreading…
The sheets got so soaked
From the passion provoked,
We had to replace all the bedding

My husband at war, I have wrote 'im
How I miss what he does to my scrotum
There's no one to stroke,
So I miss my bloke
Stroking it out of my totem

Knocked up by a trucker named Cletus,
They attempted to pull out the fetus…
'Twas all in bad form,
And when it is born,
A deformed little fella will greet us

When couples are bored and snowed in,
It's incredibly tempting to sin…
So nine months and a week
After Winter Storm Pete,
We welcomed our sweet Emma Lynn

The Limerick,
Restored

Turkey Day last year became lewd
When we gathered to eat in the nude…
Now each year we're living
A naughty Skanksgiving:
We fuck all the beautiful food

I feel such total devotion
And lovely, ecstatic emotion
To the love of my life,
My perfect young wife,
Who loves being pumped with my lotion

One fateful Fourth of July,
She sucked a Republican guy…
He was drunk on Bud Light
As his semen took flight,
Splattering right in her eye

When I feast my eyes on a chicken,
Juicy and fresh in the kitchen,
The hot, meaty poultry
Is looking so sultry,
I just wanna go stick my dick in

He forced my poor wife to bone
And soon, her womb would be grown…
His violation
Caused fertilization,
But I'll love the kid as my own

I win the hearts of my nieces
With candy like gummies and Reese's…
Once they're adoring,
It's time for the goring:
I'll fuck their sweet pussies to pieces

The Limerick,
Restored

My woman, she treats me so right,
And cooks a good supper each night,
And takes care of her bod,
So when I shove my rod,
Her pussy is perfectly tight

Raised in a rotting old shanty
By a penniless, dimwitted auntie,
I was often so bored
I'd slip her my sword,
Or sit around sniffing her panties

My sister's a dreadful young cumdump,
Where guys like to dump all their fun spunk...
But now she's all preggo
From sperm in her eggo,
And has to raise somebody's young punk

The kid stole the headmaster's chalk
To draw a big pic of a cock…
The headmaster appealed
That the perp be revealed,
But none of his classmates would talk

An unpopular fella named Herman
Most regarded as vermin…
But his wife and best friend
Stayed around 'till the end,
And always let him get his sperm in

The new girl's Ashley, or Ash,
And she's really making a splash:
In Trig 101
She made every boy cum,
And they all got a genital rash

The Limerick,
Restored

When Mama caught her boy fappin',
She ran right up and she slapped 'im…
She said, "Every boy knows
That when his weenie grows,
Only his mama should whack 'im."

I came back from years in the war,
And once she had opened our door,
My heavy load
Was so keen to explode,
I fucked my sweet wife like a whore

For a strip club marketing blitz,
'Twas the holidays, so this fits:
They put out a sign
Saying "Boys, get in line,
You'll get to see Santa's wife's tits!"

A girl became a young dyke
But then discovered she liked
Some non-human rod,
Like the one from her dog:
A fleshy, irregular spike

A princess, once she was legal,
Engaged in a tryst rather regal…
Just like Game of Thrones,
Her brother's bone
Was chomped by her wet little beagle

I got drunk and pounded my neighbor
Months later, she went into labor
The insemination
Caused colonization
Of egg from the juice of my saber

The Limerick,
Restored

The predator used Halloween
To prowl the streets for a teen...
In his costume and mask,
It's an easier task,
For it's easier not to be seen

When I need to ogle and drool,
I head to my local town pool
Hotter than all the others
Are all the young mothers,
Eager to suck on my tool

Something about slimy toads
Makes me quick to explode:
When I think of their lips
And their firm froggy grip,
I blow such a marvelous load

SECTION III:
Bestiality, Family Life, & Holidays

We've strayed so far from our God,
They make dildos from horses and dogs...
So godless babes feast
On the cock of a beast;
A rubbery animal log

When humans are in absentia,
I rely, instead, on rodentia...
It's a little bit vile
But it works for a while,
Despite vaginal differentia

A man I once knew loved to dine
On bacon, and other cooked swine...
But he loved it most raw
('Twas a sexual flaw),
For he found piggy asshole divine

The Limerick,
Restored

A lass at the zoo had some thoughts
When she saw all the chimps stroking off…
Once in the enclosure,
The monkeys disrobed her,
And quickly moved in for a boff

There was a young plumber from Prague
Whose love for his female dog
Was much more than you'd think,
For he'd plunge out her stink,
Removing most of the clog

Events became less than quotidian
When a highway-cruising Floridian
Saw in the next car,
Her legs spread with a bar,
A lady fucked by an ophidian

My soulmate, I thought, I had wed,
But now, my poor heart is dead…
Surprising sweet girlie
By coming home early,
Found her stuffed with a cock in our bed

She knew that she shouldn't get hitched
When she felt a bacterial itch
Seeing where this was heading,
She called off the wedding,
And treated her labial ditch

I know you have slept with a man
Who is also the son of your gran…
Not that I'm bothered,
But fucking your father
Is not an advisable plan

The Limerick,
Restored

I'm trying to send her a sign
That I want her as my Valentine…
Cut her name in my arm,
Which left her alarmed;
Even more when I showed her the shrine

I'm a retired old sailor
Who lives in a derelict trailer…
But I have my best pal—
A loyal old gal,
Who's happy whenever I nail 'er

A dog that I knew, cute but manic,
Self-medicated her panic:
In frustrated passion,
And frightening fashion,
She'd hump you like something Satanic

There once was a long-distance hiker,
And a bear decided he liked her…
Deep in the woods,
He gave her his goods,
And honey burst out as he spiked her

A seagull, filthy and wet,
Spread its wings in a gesture of threat
Rose up like a phoenix,
Displaying its penis:
A strange little feathered baguette

A creampie-obsessed little slut
Loved to take sperm in her gut
'Till insemination
Caused belly inflation,
As triplets were born from the nut

The Limerick,
Restored

When a gal invites you to breed,
You must deliver your seed…
So slip in your eel,
And soon she will feel
The goo she so desperately needs

A whore, big-assed but titless,
I hired to let me fuck shitless…
Her kid watched the fuck,
Which cost two hundred bucks,
And involved things that no kid should witness

Sucked right into a daze,
A fountain of masculine glaze
Was quickly consumed
From the cock of the groom,
As his bride sung a marital praise

A guy met a hot rural moaner
Who decided to not let him bone her...
But then led by the arm,
Took him back to the barn,
And offered her sis as a loaner

My reproductive man-potion
Is a potent and powerful lotion:
When I'm nice and hard,
And shoot out some lard,
A fetus is set into motion

As soon as the condom is on,
The blood will all drain from his schlong
So they fucked raw,
And soon they both saw,
She grew from the fruit of his dong

The Limerick,
Restored

Today, my joy blooms anew,
For it's sunny, and skies are so blue,
And I've got a wife
Who will fuck me for life,
And lives for the taste of my goo

Your fun, flirty friend, name of Sheri,
Says she loves being free and unmarried…
But as your family's grown,
She's still alone,
And now she's so lonely, it's scary

A vengeful old Maître d'
Seated 'em where they'd smell pee:
Outside the pisser.
And as for his kisser,
Some feces mixed in the Chablis

SECTION III:
Bestiality, Family Life, & Holidays

When first he played with my bum,
He said it would just be the thumb…
I meekly consented,
But soon so resented
The full-erect shaft and the cum

SECTION IV:
History, Politics, & Current Events

The Limerick,
Restored

Turns out that ole' General Custer
Has a cock that just doesn't pass muster:
This sad little man
Has had his Last Stand…
His cock isn't much of a buster

That Infowars tart, Millie Weaver
Has such a magnificent beaver
And as Alex Jones knows,
She loves giving blows…
An eager oral reliever

Melania ditched her rich hubby
For Trudeau, after seeing his chubby—
It pleased her much better
Than Trump's little member:
Shriveled, flaccid, and stubby

Some folks on the web think Podesta
Is a Satanic child molesta
Now with Epstein's death
It seems plausible, yes,
That they all love a pedo fiesta

To avoid prosecution, a Roman
Convinced ole' Caesar to blow 'im...
But his lordship's salami
And creamy tsunami
Proved too potent an omen

Trump practiced the art of his deal
On a prostitute who couldn't feel
His miniscule member
One night in November,
But faked it with deafening squeals

The Limerick,
Restored

The prince, an old Saudi royal
Had a cock infected with boils…
He spread them around
Fucking all in his town
And for lube, resorted to oil

An enema made of strong coffee
And sweetened lightly with toffee
Left a diplomat randy
To squirt his white candy,
In all from Merkel to Gaddhafi

At the airport, I was selected
For a pat-down quite unexpected:
TSA touched my dick,
And though I felt sick,
My penis was promptly erected

Despite her support from the gays,
Clinton lost, and entered a rage…
At the lost nomination,
She cursed all creation,
And fucked Huma into a daze

There is a small man in my pants
Who goes on political rants…
When he goes crazy,
My world gets hazy
In civic and sexual trance

A Bavarian chef was the first
To fuck a fräulein with wurst…
But he got #MeToo'd,
And presently sued
When they found the gal was coerced

The Limerick,
Restored

A soldier, just back from Iraq,
Had a curious case of shell shock:
Now back from the fray,
Had to cum every day,
And couldn't stop touching his cock

A gentrification event
Arose from the lure of cheap rent:
A hipster, ill-fated
Was perforated
With homicidal intent

Our political schism
Of communists vs. fascism
Could be solved best
With the trading of sex,
A truce out of pleasure and jism

In a village, ancient and Swedish,
A Viking was feeling quite fiendish…
With no upcoming raids,
He went looking for maids,
And bedded the first who showed cleavage

Me and the boys in the corps,
During weeks' worth of evenings at war,
Bored out of our minds,
We'd sometimes unwind
By sneaking in through the back door

An embattled leader, Germanic
Had sexual needs, rather manic:
A white, gooey geyser
Came forth from the Kaiser
During a national panic

The Limerick,
Restored

A terrible bout of The Dryness
Made barren the crotch of Her Highness
She called forth the jester,
Who'd surely molest her,
And moisten her vaginal sinus

I know of a guy, Kawashima
More heroic than Iwo Jima:
Stuck The Bomb up his ass,
Took the brunt of the blast,
And saved all of Hiroshima

The problem, it seems, is quite vast:
The women are being harassed
A spank, a smooch,
A thumb up the cooch,
Even when they didn't ask

100

When she finished up her audition,
The producer said, "It's tradition…
You're great for the part,
But before we start,
You'll suck my cock to fruition."

Un hombre conosco, muy feo:
"Solo cojo modelas, yo creo."
Fue una mentira,
Por que nadie admira
Una cara como Michael Pompeo

Things were even more rapey
Back in the 90s and 80s:
Wankers and hams
With their dicks in their hands,
Groping most all of the ladies

The Limerick,
Restored

When King Arthur is feeling quite bored,
An object is sure to be gored
This hump-crazy punk
Is dumping his spunk
Wherever he buries his sword

In the case of Qassem Soleimani,
He was pounded by Trump's big salami
Trump had plenty to prove,
So he had him removed,
And sent him to cry to his mommy

I live in a rapey regime
With laws that are rather extreme:
Required by law
For people bourgeois,
Is to worship the dictator's cream

There once was a sheikh in Riyadh
And for sex, he traveled abroad
But his best secret lover,
I'd later discover,
Was his rival, Bashar al-Assad

The power of Dr. Einstein
Wasn't his big thinking mind
His genius imbued
In his balls, big and blue,
Pondering mass, space, and time

The great mind of math, Dr. Euler
Took his lab tech down by the boiler
He whipped up a graph
To angle his staff,
Delivering fluid to soil 'er

The Limerick,
Restored

The court ruled against both his testicles,
And ruined his seminal vesicles:
To shut off his stuff,
They cut off his nuts, and
Ensure that no kids are accessible

In Berlin, where the Nazis had risen,
'Twas a Master Race they envisioned…
So when you're The Fuhrer,
Nothing is purer
Than Aryan cum for the mission

At the obscenity trial,
They ruled that my limericks were vile
And said, 'cause my writing
Is too uninviting,
I ought to be jailed a while

The Democrats can't take my gun!
It protects me, and it's so much fun…
'Cause when it is loaded,
And sexually goaded,
It shoots fifty-caliber cum

I was pinned down by Charlie in 'Nam,
And hit by the blast of a bomb…
With my balls in a crater,
'Twas even worse later
When my dick was blown off by Saddam

Some news from a local rest area
Is causing a local hysteria:
They say for the gays,
It's the place where they play,
Spreading their homo malaria

The Limerick,
Restored

Turned in by a victim named Helen,
For sneaking a honk of her melons,
I was arrested,
For gals I molested,
And now am a sexual felon

My semen is biodegradable,
But the climate effects are debatable
I do not know,
With each load I blow,
Whether I'm being sustainable

I am a servant, indentured
But my life is a sexy adventure:
I tend to the fief,
Then suck off my chief;
The overlord, he's quite a drencher

When she thinks about fucking police,
It works up her vaginal grease…
So away she is sneaking
To tend to her leaking,
And finger herself to release

I'm serving some hard prison time
For things I expressed in my rhymes…
So what if they're lewd,
Offensive, or crude?
I didn't know art was a crime

With president Vermin Supreme,
My teeth are impeccably clean
We all got a pony
(I use mine to blow me,)
And our country's as great as I've seen

The Limerick,
Restored

The commander and schemer, Obama,
Hatched a plan to catch ole' Osama:
Lure him out with some ass,
But don't use a lass:
He'd rather a goat or a llama

I stood before a stern jury
Which convicted me in a hurry...
For I found someone dead,
To give me some head,
And pump full of seminal slurry

In a Soweto favela,
I saw the great Nelson Mandela...
He was nude in a hut,
His thumb up his butt,
Sucking a muscular fella

A protest in dozens of cities
Has women revealing their titties…
As a man, I applaud
The politicized bod,
Even with tits itty-bitty

I'm not sure who I should blame
For making society tame…
Whether left or the right,
There's no end in sight
To things being sterile and lame

I'm a full-blown chauvinist bastard,
And love to pump women with plaster…
But times have sure changed
For fellas deranged—
#MeToo is a total disaster

The Limerick,
Restored

Although I am ugly and gaunt,
It's confidence that I flaunt...
I'm like Casanova,
So they will bend ovah—
I fuck any girl I want

What recently passed as just rude
Could now quickly get you #MeToo'd...
Now the gals get their say
On which men go away,
Turning rapists to docile prudes

Bill Clinton, a known luminary
Has done so much raping, it's scary...
A #MeToo he's dodged,
Despite what he lodged
Into women who he'd never marry

There once was a king, name of Tut
Deformed from his skull to his gut
That's just the way
Of nature, they say,
When you're born from incestuous nut

"We're losing our climate change mission,"
They say, though it's just superstition…
It's all pseudoscience,
The bastards are lyin',
To tax all my phallic emissions

A supple, well-formed Roman sentry
Met an equite, borne of the gentry
He said, "None shall pass,"
But he yielded fast,
When the knight plugged his gluteal entry

The Limerick,
Restored

The *real* swamp of D.C.
Is one that you'll never see,
Where children are traded
Like cards 'till they're faded;
Ghosts in the Land of the Free

Prince Andrew is finally disgraced
But the music, he still hasn't faced
For he hasn't been jailed,
'Cause justice has failed
The lives to which he's laid waste

I was indicted for being perverted
For the liquid my penis had squirted…
But the pertinent question is,
Was there aggression,
And where was the penis inserted?

My wealth, it lends me immunity
For raping in my community:
Though everyone knows,
My money still flows,
And so, I can rape with impunity

An intern with D.C. ambitions
Aroused some spousal suspicions…
A P.I. filmed the governor,
Sweaty and lovin'er,
Sinking the doomed politician

The sight of a puckered brown bud
Caused an urge in a cave-dwelling stud:
Each species and sex,
(Even T-Rex)
Was sodomized 'till he saw blood

The Limerick,
Restored

There once was an ancient Peruvian
With outbursts, abrupt and vesuvian…
He'd scream while he stroked,
Scaring the folks
In his town, antediluvian

I once knew girl named Deena,
Who I'd sometimes fuck with my wienah…
One day she declined,
But I missed the signs,
And now I've been served a subpoena

There was a politician named Tulsi,
Whose tight little body was dolci:
Hot little Gabbard
Can suck on my scabbard,
Her eyes looking sexy and sultry

Evil and smooth was a dude
Whose interest in rape was quite lewd…
Got away with them all,
For he's rich, white, and tall,
And also quite legally shrewd

I once knew a dancer, exotic
With a fantasy rather quixotic…
With a dream, presidential,
The gal had potential
To fight for our freedoms, erotic

A very well-fucked ancient cumslut
Drew on the caves lots of cum smut…
Archaeologists, later,
And museum curators,
Studied her drawings of cum nut

The Limerick,
Restored

The ancient Greek god known as Hermes
Relied on his little Greek wormy
His message did land
Once it shot from his gland;
A memo so white and so spermy

There shall be cruel consequences
For sexual crimes and offenses:
Make all the brutes
Eat a steel-toe boot,
And then they will come to their senses

There once was a gal from Verona
Who contracted the virus, corona:
A fella from China
Fucked her vagina
With his diseased little bonah

SECTION V:
Identity Politics, Sexuality, & Gender

The Limerick,
Restored

A parent seeking Woke cred
Announced her old child was dead:
"Behold all the splendor,
My child's new gender,
Re-birthed now from Jenna to Jed!"

A most awkward gender revealing
Gave all a discomforting feeling...
Mom announced from the bed,
"It's a *girl*," she said,
Though the penis damn near reached the ceiling

A financier in Pompeii
Suspected a client was gay...
He almost confessed
Feelings he too possessed,
But the volcano blew them away

Born a cisgender male,
I ate too much soy and kale…
My dick dropped right off,
And I'm silky and soft,
'Cause now I am fully female

Convincingly feminized,
I'm a hottie in many men's eyes,
Their stares never wider
When they think "Now I'll ride her,"
And find what's enclosed in my thighs

A skinny, effeminate twink
Goes by he/him ('least I think)
It matters no bit
If it's got some tits,
A weenie, some nuts, or a pink

The Limerick,
Restored

A delicate feminist male
In romance, predictably failed
While gals liked his sweetness,
They scoffed at the weakness
With which he would paddle their tails

A lady, extremely androgynous,
Tickles my places, erogenous
"If I like it," I say,
"Am I mildly gay?"
I'm concerned with arousal endogenous

I once knew a hot in-betweener
With such a sultry demeanor…
While their gender perplexed me,
Their face was so sexy,
Regardless if they had a wiener

I donned my transgender disguise
To feast on the visual prize:
In the ladies' room lockers,
Bare asses and knockers;
A libertine feast for the eyes

It's okay if some of your progeny
Display a few signs of androgyny...
The kids will be fine,
So don't lose your mind
Over a lack of homogeny

Little boys who enjoy wearing dresses
Need not be subjected to stresses
He's only four,
So let him explore—
But cherish the nuts he possesses

The Limerick,
Restored

What a curious modern amenity
To assume a new gender identity:
"I must present
As a masculine gent,
Or I'll never feel serenity."

My personal sexual world
Reaches beyond boys and girls…
I'll fuck sissies and trannies,
And wrinkly grannies,
A corgi, or even a squirrel

Being labeled as gay was his fear,
So in ballet, he felt rather queer…
But he showed such aplomb
When they learned contretemps,
The girls were hot for his gear

Dad didn't support my ballet,
And said as I danced through the hallway:
"My own son, a fag,"
But I showed that old bag,
Becoming the darling of Broadway

Three bullies surrounded young Larry:
"You twink," "You faggot," "You fairy!"
Yet, two out of three
Were gayer than he,
Preferring some meat to a cherry

When girls you know become Woke,
Just give em' a penile poke—
Despite your offenses,
They'll come to their senses
From orgasm penis provokes

The Limerick,
Restored

When you are irreparably Woke,
You can't take a joke for a joke…
You become just a vulture,
Picking at culture,
Until it's irreparably broke

I once knew a young dullard thespian
Who converted a rather butch lesbian
He dazzled her true
With his cock-hammer goo,
For his intellect proved quite pedestrian

My parents have sent me away
To a curative camp for the gays
They say it's a curse
To be queer on this earth,
But I don't believe what they say

The gays conspired conversion
To turn Glen to a female version…
But their homo agenda
To turn Glen into Glenda
Was countered with fear and revulsion

Some whore drilled a hole in the wall,
For fellas to come drain their balls…
And for pleasure down south,
It don't matter what mouth—
It could be a guy or a doll

I'd fuck lesbos, bi's and the gays,
And they love my pansexual ways…
But I don't stop at that,
Fuck a shrew and a cat;
Whatever I find that obeys

The Limerick,
Restored

I'm deeply in lust with a man,
Hungry after his hands…
I'll let him slip in
My warm, slippery skin
To tickle my masculine glands

My uncle, dressed like a queen,
Was the best thing my sisters had seen…
But my father would say,
"It's incredibly gay,"
And convince us that it was unclean

I've traveled across all the lands
To fuck all the men who are trans:
Pretty-dick girls
Are my whole world,
And I am their biggest of fans

I once knew a gay little bootblack—
A twink who loved getting ass-packed
When short of a bear
For an anal affair,
He'll settle for sucking some black sack

An androgynous lass, name of Gloria,
Experienced gender dysphoria…
Obsessed with her dream
Of a cock that shoots cream,
And other such phantasmagoria

Women, I think, should be free,
To be what they want to be…
The freer they get,
The better the bet
They'll fuck any fella they see

The Limerick,
Restored

His father, so set in his ways,
Was shocked when his son joined the gays…
Little did the son know,
His dad used to blow
During his boarding school days

There are many ways to do lesbian sex,
It depends on which way you like best
But for straight, horny men,
The sole question is when
You will get FMF sex requests

SECTION VI:
Scatalogical, Vomit, & Anal Play

The Limerick,
Restored

A celiac diagnosee
Had to eat everything gluten-free,
So just one little bit
Of wheat in his grits
Had him shitting out vile debris

A girl who liked to eat shit
And spread it all over her tits
Got a bad UTI
When a shit-loving guy
Ate her cunt after licking her nips

I once knew a gal, name of Sue
Many-a man she would do
Her limit did come
When one entered her bum,
And she found spots of blood in her poo

SECTION VI:
Scatalogical, Vomit, & Anal Play

I once knew a passionate foodie
Who liked to take fruit in her bootie…
She just drew the line
At a big slice of lime,
And a pineapple rammed in the beauty

A pregnant gal's passion for anal
Tragically, proved to be fatal:
The hole of her anus
Was pounded so heinous,
It aborted a being prenatal

There was a kayaker named Doug
Who paddled so fast, he was smug…
He had a queer trick,
Small, round, and slick:
His dependable racing butt plug

The Limerick,
Restored

A unique and organic purée
Was the focus of all of her play:
Have a date? Bring a scoop,
For this gal's into poop,
And will savor your rectal sorbet

A poo slave I know, name of Lilly,
Is oftentimes forced to eat chili:
Her Dom likes observing
The poo she is serving,
While she is sucking his willy

She moved into a building for rent,
But no rent money ever was sent...
She paid with her pooper,
Letting the super
Fill her with sticky cement

Scatalogical, Vomit, & Anal Play

My burbling, brown fecal thunder
Is causing some others to wonder—
Soon, the whole pool
Will be brown from my stool,
In a gastrointestinal blunder

When I took my seat on the lieu,
My hot liquid shits were beaucoup…
They burned my Brown Betty,
Making me sweaty,
Clenching with pain from poo-poo

His top food, other than cereal,
Was vile fecal material…
Though he finally quit
All his gobbling shit,
He died of infection, bacterial

The Limerick,
Restored

When I took a big shit in the ocean,
Events were set into motion:
My foul inner beef
Extinguished the reefs
Damaged by sun-blocking lotion

A drunk and loose-pussied old townie
Let me cum into her brownie…
She stayed in the city
To show off her titties
To every last guy in the county

I sat myself down for a think
About how to pummel a stink:
Will my dick tear her butt?
Does this make her a slut?
Should I wash afterwards in the sink?

SECTION VI:
Scatalogical, Vomit, & Anal Play

My girlfriend says I'm a chicken
For being afraid of butt lickin'…
But the thought of my tongue
Stuck deep in a bum
Does leave me feeling quite sickened

There is nothing as vile or base
As puking all over a face…
But for some, it's a gas
To hurl and blast
Their chunkies all over the place

When sphincter muscles are weak,
Your anus is likely to leak—
Work out your excreter,
Or you'll leak a liter,
Becoming a shit-leaking freak

The Limerick,
Restored

Suzie's particular kink
For things buried deep in her stink
Made her brown pooper
A bit of a drooper,
But it will recover (I think)

I gaze upon your brown fundament
With lust, and starry-eyed wonderment…
Wanna give you a ride
So I feel inside,
Injecting a liquidy supplement

I wanted a little brown morsel,
So I entered her organ most dorsal…
She enjoyed it enough,
But said 'twas too rough—
So next time I won't be as forceful

SECTION VI:
Scatalogical, Vomit, & Anal Play

Some proctological trouble
Involving a massive gas bubble
Couldn't be more succinct
As it emptied my stink
In about a half-gallon of rubble

Minutes after I'm mugged,
I find that I'm anally plugged:
The horrible thief,
He stuffed me with beef,
Using his seminal slug

Once you are old and quite creaky,
I'm afraid that your butt becomes leaky
But if you're not aware,
You can buy underwear
To catch all the drips from your cheekies

The Limerick,
Restored

Is there a thing as absurd
As an anus, squeezing a turd?
And the sound of the plop
As you squeeze out your slop
Is the funniest music I've heard

Now that my butthole's distended,
My anal career has been ended…
An excess of lust,
And too forceful a thrust,
Caused damage that cannot be mended

You know, if you have met us,
We love to shred rectal lettuce…
We'll shred yours too,
But if there is poo,
It will severely upset us

SECTION VI:
Scatalogical, Vomit, & Anal Play

A deposit at the ole' Bank of Fudge
Left my cock with an unseemly smudge…
But I wiped off the poo,
And looked good as new;
No reason to carry a grudge

On a date with a girl named Mia,
She was stricken by bad diarrhea…
I forgave it at first,
'Till one of the bursts
Ruined the back of my Kia

My date farted putrescent vapor,
And I simply couldn't escape her:
We were both trapped inside
An amusement park ride,
Breathing the gas of her gaper

The Limerick,
Restored

At a dingy rest stop in Toledo,
I squeezed out a fecal torpedo…
When some guy had the gall,
Through a hole in the wall,
To insert erectile meat-o

A millionaire in Manassas
Was haunted by furious gasses…
His farts were so noxious,
They scared off the foxes,
Leaving the fattest of lasses

A girl's gravelly speaking,
She blamed on flu season peaking…
But 'twas a fetish for barf,
And choking with scarves,
That caused her guttural creaking

SECTION VI:
Scatalogical, Vomit, & Anal Play

A woman swore off all the guys
For all their limp dicks and their lies…
But then she met one
Whose tongue, in her bum,
Was the ultimate masculine prize

For a man with a bad GI tract,
His farts were a troublesome fact…
Gals'd say, "What's, that smell—
Oh, it's *you?* Jesus hell!"
And like that, his confidence cracked

An unfortunate gluteal boil
Forced a young laddie to toil,
For the puss and the blood,
They came in a flood,
Along with his gluteal soil

The Limerick,
Restored

Lavatorial duties
Are reality, even for cuties,
But their inner coal
Smells like cinnamon rolls
As it comes out of their booties

A glorious hole in my city
Became momentarily unpretty:
With a rectum asunder,
And brown of down under,
Results were predictably shitty

To my horror, while getting laid,
My ass blew a brownish grenade
I however, by fate,
Had a shit-loving mate,
Who wasn't the least bit dismayed

'Twas the Lordship of King Robert Zachary
When he lorded over the factory
Making synthetic farts
As a strange work of art,
To dazzle the senses olfactory

I once dated a kinkster named Pearl,
Who loved when I forced her to hurl…
But my cock down her larynx
Disappointed her parents,
Ashamed of their puke-loving girl

Here is a fucking technique
I learned from my girl this week:
After plunging her butt,
You must keep it shut—
Once loosened, it's likely to leak

The Limerick,
Restored

This lecher I know, name of Todd
Was always stuffing his wad…
At parties, too plugged,
He'd bleed on my rug—
But usually, nobody saw

I feel my little heart sink
When she won't let me into her stink…
The exiting hole
Is ideal for pole,
'Cause it's tighter than her little pink

I'm mostly sexy as hell,
But my farts have a terrible smell…
If I want to fuck her,
I'll have to pucker,
So all of my gasses are quelled

SECTION VI:
Scatalogical, Vomit, & Anal Play

To access her feminine fruit,
You must puncture her vaginal chute
If you bore of the pussy,
Switch to her tushie;
There's always a bootie to loot

My cum has soaked all of my towels,
So I've nothing to mop up my bowels
This issue of laundry
Has me in a quandary:
My house is alarmingly foul

SECTION VII:
Geography, Ethnicity, & Adventure

The Limerick,
Restored

'Twas a group of Italian gays
Rather rough in their sexual ways…
So a squirting tornado
Of ass-bound Alfredo
Caused leakage of butt Bolognese

A spring breaker I met in Cancún
Had no undies to cover her poon…
We got rather drunk,
So my fingers could dunk
Knuckle-deep once we went to my room

A droopy-eyed, pervy Venetian
Was known for unwelcome secretions…
Thus a gay gondolier,
Despite being queer,
Had to dodge his wank to completion

Geography, Ethnicity, & Adventure

I took a strange foreign injection,
Inducing an epic erection…
It lasted nine years,
Eliciting jeers,
And sometimes, unwanted affection

A tailor I knew in Pamplona
Couldn't stop the growth of his bonah…
His footlong found fame,
But never a dame
It fucked without causing a coma

A muscled young Greek met a cutie,
And entranced by his tanned, bubble bootie,
She moaned in delight,
Groped his cheeks good and tight—
Unaroused, it turned out he was fruity

The Limerick,
Restored

A shrink out in Constantinople
Had to treat a Mercurian yokel:
"I'm the god of all fortune,
But admit, it is torture
To shit out pure diamonds and opal!"

An usurious lender from Cairo
Defrauded an Aegean pyro…
The psycho returned,
Used the bank as it burned,
To cook the crook's cock for a gyro

I once knew a daring young phallus;
A sailor, erect on the ballast…
His cock waved a flag
From the skin of his sag,
And the wind caused his balls to be calloused

Met a gambling harlot in Vegas
So dirty, that no church could save us…
I blame local temptation,
And excess libations,
For nasty desires that plague us

When white cock and black pussy are stacked,
It looks like an Oreo snack…
But this time the cream
Goes on her brown bean,
Or maybe all over her back

A virgin, alone and pathetic,
Became rather peripatetic…
He traveled the land,
His dick in his hand;
A pussy-hunting ascetic

The Limerick,
Restored

Lost in her pure delectation,
A gal of Bavarian station
Was fucked by the Rhine
About forty times,
With lots of orgasmic causation

I went to the strait of Hormuz
To pay for this mean little cooz—
T'was the wife of the king,
Such a small nasty thing,
Sent away for sleeping with Jews!

I wanted to visit each state,
In each I would masturbate…
But in cold Alaska,
My cum turned to plaster,
And jammed up my little prostate

A Jew I once knew, quite neurotic,
Could be cured by a dancer, exotic:
Forgot all his worries,
All because Murray
Was finding the titties hypnotic

On a birthday trip to Manhattan,
A fella's Big Apple was fattened
When a fine birthday slurp
Made him squirt all his gurt;
That is exactly what happened

There once was a Haudenosaunee
Who desperately wanted to bone me
I was eager to wash
Her corn, beans, and squash
With my vascular pony

The Limerick,
Restored

A Manchester slag getting faded
One night at the pub, was invaded
    With pluggings persistent,
    And a strain most resistant,
She wished she had just masturbated

The cartographer, lonely at mast,
Mapping the world at last,
    Would often get bored,
    Land to find whores,
And navigate straight to their ass

In First Class, your stewardess might
Come up to your seat on the flight
    To deliver your peanuts,
    And suck on your penis,
So you can sleep all through the night

The first time I tasted a taco,
I was still joven y flaco,
But far from Oaxaca,
I traveled for soccer,
And fucked a young gal in Morocco

After my anesthesia,
I had a case of amnesia…
My asshole was stretched,
And it seems far-fetched,
But I woke in a town in Tunisia

Did you hear of the Tit Man, from Ipswich?
He had a big pair of bitch tits…
He gives them a jiggle,
And everyone giggles,
And gives a wee pinch to his bitch nips

The Limerick,
Restored

This gal I knew in Beijing
Used her cunt to blow smoke rings
But when she gave birth,
It threw off her girth,
And now her cunt's just a birth thing

The best thing about dating French?
You already know they're a wench:
They'll fuck any ole' smoker
As long as you'll poke her,
And aren't afraid of the stench

I once knew a gal from Belize
Who was quite the indelible tease:
Though she flashed me her pea
On a tropical caye,
My lusting would not be appeased

At the party, a well-hung Latino
Had a penis that bulged through his chinos…
El serpiente,
Obviamente,
Got hard when he drank too much vino

An uncouth and boorish Hungarian
Became rather sick and vulgarian:
Always basking in whores,
With cum on the floor,
And dripping in juices ovarian

Girls who are Japanese
Love to flirt and to giggle and tease,
And since girls so Asian
Love fucking Caucasians,
I slip in their panties with ease

The Limerick,
Restored

There was a 600-pound Russian
With a fondness for sexual crushing…
Despite all I pled,
She smothered me dead,
Without any further discussion

I eat at the finest hotels
To seduce the finest of belles…
In the Bellagio,
One sucked the formaggio
Out of my sweaty morel

I bedded a sexy young Greek
Washing her clothes by the creek…
This babe of Byzantium,
I sucked her chrysanthemum,
And let her explore my physique

I met a young man in Siam
Whose cock was as wide as a can:
My face stretched around it,
He thrust and he pounded,
And now I need a brain scan

Desperately seeking some warmth
In the coldest lands on the earth,
A pudendal packet
Is warm as a jacket,
When you are horny up north

The King of the land Yogyakarta
Was caught with a boy in Jakarta…
They wanted him dead,
So the pervert-king fled,
Hiding in Puerto Vallarta

The Limerick,
Restored

A seafaring skank was out gloating
Regarding her skills at the throating…
To prove it was fact,
She hurriedly packed
The rod that the captain was toting

On a seaworthy passenger liner,
The stewardess couldn't be finer:
Her tits said "Ahoy!"
So I made her my toy,
Docking right in her vaginer

My quest is a horn-dogging hunt
For the finest, divinest of cunts…
And when they are found,
I'll give em' a pound,
Using my masculine shunt

Down at the swampy old bog,
Fucking is kind of a slog:
Conditions are harsh
Down in the marsh,
Deep in the mud with the frogs

Each winter, I flee from the freeze
By flying myself to Belize…
Then I hit the beach,
And it's women I seek,
To give all their titties a squeeze

The women of ole' Tora Bora
Are so kind, they'll put it in for ya:
They'll grab your dong,
If it's short or long,
And point to their vaginal flora

The Limerick,
Restored

We were on a one-hundred pitch climb,
Having one hell of a time:
On pitch sixty-nine
I tickled her 'gine,
And sucked out some vaginal slime

A ribald old mountaineer
Realized he was a queer...
He hoped to get fisted,
But the Sherpa resisted,
And ended his climbing career

Nearly all of the Asians
Were forged from the Mongol invasion:
Mongolian breeding
Quickly was leading
To quite the genetic occasion

This Indian gal, a Shoshone,
Happily kneeled below me
She wanted my beads,
So we did nasty deeds;
I paid her some wampum to blow me

A horny teen boy from Calcutta,
His semen was smoother than butta…
He had a fine dick,
But he couldn't score chicks,
On account of he spoke with a stutta

After I'm thrown overboard,
I say to myself, "Please Lord…"
Then I wash ashore,
And am saved by a whore,
Who lovingly nurses my sword

The Limerick,
Restored

There was a young lady from Bend
Who started an interesting trend:
She sold the secretion
Of orgasmic completion,
With flavors you can't comprehend

Me and my buddy, Vihan,
Were happily getting it on:
He blew his paneer
All over my ears,
Then sucked the dahl from my wand

A gunslinger, name of Juanito,
Loved sucking a juicy taquito…
The hot desperado
Got caught in the grotto,
And Sheriff made sure he was frito

There once was a sexual tourist
Who was naturally horny and whorish…
From Red Rocks to Acadia,
She pleasured her labia,
And loved being fucked in the forest

Sipping a beer in Havana,
In a nice little beachside cabana,
A gal at the bar,
She smoked my cigar,
And sat on my meaty banana

The best thing about all the Brits?
They'll readily show you their tits!
Take em' out to the pub,
And they'll lend you a rub
As you fill up their vaginal bits

The Limerick,
Restored

A trafficker in Cozumel
Was looking for pussy to sell…
He dangled his lure
Down in Punta Sur,
And snatched up a tart named Michelle

When Paloma was sucking my pollo,
She was bobbing her head like a yo-yo…
In her home ciudad,
She was sucking my rod,
And licking up all of my fro-yo

A gunslingin' gal, Henrietta
Kneeled to suck my Beretta…
As the clock struck high noon
At the Tombstone Saloon,
She sucked out a glob of my feta

SECTION VII:
Geography, Ethnicity, & Adventure

I try, when I'm sightseein',
To fuck a gal European:
From Budapest to Berlin,
I'll give em' a spin,
As long as they are agreein'

A hooker I fucked in Madrid
Showed up with a couple of kids…
They waited out front
While I pounded her cunt,
Which the Lord strictly forbids

A Cheyenne brought me into her teepee,
To suck on my little white peepee…
Then her clan leader watched
While I hammered her crotch,
Which I thought was a little bit creepy

The Limerick,
Restored

My worldly friend, name of Bobby,
Will only fuck girls Punjabi:
They go out for curry,
They suck out his slurry,
And this is his cultural hobby

I enjoy the Caribbean breeze
As the island gal gets on her knees...
The best part of vacation
Is beachside fellation,
Which often results in disease

A climber suffered through hell
When he fucked a gal on rappel:
The thrust of his wiener
Unscrewed the 'biner
And then, the two lovers fell

I knew a black gal in Crown Heights
Who dressed up on most of her nights
Cruising the town,
Sexy and brown,
Fucking most all of the whites

A hooker I knew in Korea
Did a trick with her vaginal pita:
Her squirt was a plume
That could cross the whole room;
A hose of her warm blennorrhea

My days are a horn-dogging journey,
A life that's so slutty and whory…
I get such delight
From a pussy each night,
To celebrate coital glory

The Limerick,
Restored

A Greek bitch in ole' Santorini
Slobbered and slurped on my weenie...
My size is quite meager,
And yet, she was eager,
Even though I am so teenie

I met a young lassie in Naas
Whose tits made a powerful case…
My lust she had sensed,
So my cum was dispensed,
All over her titties and face

Geared up and seeking his daughter,
By god, he did it—he got her!
Snatched her back from a pimp,
Who he snapped like a shrimp,
Plus the punks who he scalped in the slaughter

Her legs were long like a gazelle,
And her rack made my seed blaster swell:
This femme out in France,
She got right in my pants,
And drank all my sweet béchamel

A pale young tailor from Paris
Revealed his skin was the fairest:
His pants tore a seam,
Revealing his beans,
Leaving him deeply embarrassed

Now that my sweetheart is gone,
I won't remain here for long…
I'll search far and wide
For a sexy new bride
To pound with my glorious schlong

SECTION VIII:
Religion & Authority

The Limerick,
Restored

A monk at a temple for Buddhists
Was tempted by visiting nudists…
Took himself to nirvana,
And ruined his karma,
With acts of terrible crudeness

A mensch, on his first Lucky Night,
Wore his "yarmulke" dreadfully tight…
His kishka, engorged,
Nearly burst from the force
Of the seed of the Israelite

A priest, name of old Father Castor,
Was caught in a tryst with the pastor…
With the Lord as their witness,
Both were left shitless
From rectal-ripping disaster

A soldier, loyal to orders,
Still gasped when, alone in his quarters,
Sarge entered his bunk,
Delivered his spunk,
And said, "Salute your exploiter!"

On the peak of Holy Mt. Shasta,
'Twas a numinous pot-smoking Rasta,
His "joint" being smoked
By disciples he groped,
High on his seminal salsa

I once knew a daring young teacher
Who liked to reveal his creature
To students astounded
By what they had found—
They had seen this before from their preacher

175

The Limerick,
Restored

At the briss, Rabbi damaged the youth—
Cut off his whole dick, that's the truth...
Now instead of a pole,
The kid has a hole,
So they changed him from Reuben to Ruth

A college instructor professed
His erection caused by a dress
Worn by a student
Who, rather prudent,
Kept her desires suppressed

A monk did study The Way
To determine how not to be gay...
He pulled every trick
To avoid sucking dick,
But still sucks them to this very day

There once was a Japanese swami
Known for his massive salami…
With mantras monastic,
And moves quite gymnastic,
He creamed out a massive tsunami

A girl, feeling quite whory,
Committed a rape statutory:
He said he was older—
In fact, even told her
He'd take her for sushi and nori

A judge with one fatal flaw
Failed to uphold the law:
When defendants showed cleavage,
Or hints of their beavage,
Acquitting, he'd call it a draw

The Limerick,
Restored

A hot New Age gal, with her crystal,
Used it on her new mister…
The juju convoked
Made them quite freaky folks,
So they had a three-way with her sister

Receiving an underage unit,
A teacher fucked one of her students…
She got half the sentence,
When she showed repentance,
As men for the same old imprudence

A line cook's female cleft
Was abused every night by the chef:
With a spatula slap
And a finger, the chap
Nearly diddled the girl to death

A guy who I know, called The Pope
Had a problem when Cardinals groped
Many-a youth,
And as folks learned the truth,
They got out the pitchforks and rope

For one gal, fertilization
Was a primary fixation
She was a Catholic,
So thought it not drastic
To take many spousal donations

A spiritual gal, she was fasting
But each night, her boyfriend was blasting
His glop down her throat,
Feeding masculine oats,
So her fast wasn't very long-lasting

The Limerick,
Restored

I knew an OB/GYN
Whose career came fast to an end
When they found the creep's vials
(He filled with a smile),
Of harvested vaginal phlegm

A froy who just couldn't keep kosher
Had a problem when Rabbi came over:
She sucked on his swine,
And then drank his brine,
And then he would tickle her clover

When it comes to a beach bum named Anne,
The Lord has a glorious Plan:
Righteous God willing,
I'll stuff her with filling,
And savor the juice of her clam

Coach found me alone by my locker
Said "Kid, you're a helluva blocker."
And then I would know
The price that a pro
Must pay to make it in soccer

After winning Employee of the Year,
He took her for bouchée and beer…
But her boss's true scheme
Was to give her his cream,
Forcing a grind and a smear

I once knew a doctor of note
In the field of ear, nose, and throat…
And he had a "cure"
For girls demure
Who wouldn't swallow his scrote

The Limerick,
Restored

An elder, bathed by a nurse…
His heart went from bad straight to worse:
The thing in his chest
Died when her caress
Moved to his seminal purse

The thing about church that is scary
Are the thoughts that I have about Mary:
All I can see
Is her on her knees,
Slurping my dangling berries

When Adam came into the world,
He had only the choice of one girl…
When he got bored with Eve,
Some folks believe,
He gave the Serpent a whirl

182

The legend of Mary of Nazareth
Asserts a conception, immaculate…
But I have the impression
A Roman fuck session
Delivered the Jesus ejaculate

A warrior-monk sat and wished
To learn the Way of the Fist:
This gay samurai
Lusted after a guy
To plunge all the way to his wrist

The thrill of penile implantation
Leads to eternal damnation…
Sex is immoral,
So just stick to oral,
And plenty of hard masturbation

The Limerick,
Restored

The dirtiest kind of karate
Is a martial art for the naughty:
This tae kwon do
Ends with a blow
On the meatiest part of your body

It's her first day of ole' Driver's Ed
With the teacher, a drooler named Ted...
When secluded off far,
He turns off the car,
And it fills her with terrible dread

For a teacher who needs to get laid,
It's as simple as offering grades:
To advance through his classes,
They're bouncing their asses,
In ways that their parents forbade

Desperate to fuck her professor,
She became quite the scantily dresser…
When her dress made him hard,
It lowered his guard,
And *she* became the aggressor

At St. Patrick's, a horny old saint
Was part of a dire complaint:
There was a sneak-in
When he pinned the deacon,
And made him suck sweat off his taint

A professor, handsome at school,
Caused a submissive to drool:
When she thought of him choking,
Her panties were soaking…
She flunked so he'd punish her jewel

The Limerick,
Restored

Of all the Good Lord's designs,
The pussy is top of the line:
When gals rock their hips
With a coochie that grips,
The milking is something divine

Sometimes, it's a friend of the family,
A stepdad, a teacher, or nanny…
What evil lurks
In the hearts of these jerks,
Their abuses so grim and uncanny?

I unearthed the sacred old texts
Revealing the secrets of sex:
To be harder and moister,
Eat cayenne and oysters,
And give your kegels a flex

SECTION VIII:
Religion & Authority

Aaron, brother of Moses,
Wasn't known for his fondness of hoses,
But he loved sucking rod!
It's amazing, by God,
The truths that the Devil exposes

This babe who I met at the diner
Is proof of a Godly designer:
Her tits were like clouds,
And after we plowed,
I'd never fuck something diviner

My pastor has some misgivings
About the way I've been living:
I fucked my kids' nanny,
And even their granny,
Last year at the family Thanksgiving

The Limerick,
Restored

Who knew, at a church for the Baptists,
You could get so much sexual practice?
But late nights with the pastor,
I was pumped full of plaster,
In acts that were horribly tactless

I was pulled over by a hot Statie:
Officer Anna McGrady
This sexy State Trooper,
I entered her pooper,
And now she's my butt-fucking lady

Just remember to live, laugh, and love,
And take cock in your tight little dove…
The Coexist sticker
Means you can dick her—
As willed by my God up above

SECTION VIII:
Religion & Authority

The ultimate prize, it is fabled,
Is bagging some pussy disabled…
If she has the Down's,
You can give her a pound,
But a criminal you will be labeled

When I'm King, it shall be a law
That the gals mustn't wear any bra
So from west to the east,
The fellas can feast—
Except when they visit their Ma

I worship the feminine spirit,
But only 'cause I really fear it:
When a big bitch is pissed,
Get out of its midst,
And avoid being anywhere near it

The Limerick,
Restored

I knew a sadistic young pimp
Whose dick was constantly limp
Took it out on his hoes
With insults and blows,
Ashamed of his sad little shrimp

Jesus, a very pure being,
Cannot believe what he's seeing:
His mother, sweet Mary,
Her pussy so hairy,
Rubbing herself while she's peeing

Poor, traumatized Tatiana
Sought help from a widely-known lama…
But the old Rinpoche
Would leave her betrayed
With a new and terrible drama

SECTION VIII:
Religion & Authority

Groped by a touchy employer,
I filed a suit to destroy her…
But felt fearful and torn
At the law firm one morn,
Coerced to suck on my lawyer

When she learned of the crimes of her doctor,
The scope of it all rather shocked her…
What if her dentist
And his apprentice
Made it their business to knock her?

Now with my Scorpio rising,
There's a plan that my cock is devising:
Ascending, my penis
Will penetrate Venus
For a horoscope rather surprising

The Limerick,
Restored

A scientist named Dr. Brett
Gives a student his little pipette…
His research concludes
That she looks better nude
Than most scientists he has met

I fucked an autist, once,
Who communicated in grunts…
But boy, did she moan
The moment I loaned
My cock to her autistic cunt

Judging by how they behave,
Most sinners aren't worth it to save…
We've sunk to a level
That pleases the Devil,
With all that we sexually crave

Her hubby ran off with some monks,
And she badly missed all of his spunk…
The situation was delicate,
For he'd become celibate,
And now their poor marriage has sunk

I'm sorry, but if you're a homo,
Touching my crotch is a no-no…
Told it to my rabbi,
Who tried to grab I,
And now they have jailed the Shlomo

A very young piece of jailbait
Sat at the bar with a male date…
But the bar wouldn't serve
This pedo and perv
And warned him, "You're goin' to jail, mate."

The Limerick,
Restored

In the words of a prophet,
"It's coming, and no one can stop it:
A psycho named Jan
With your nut in your hand,
Squeezing so hard that she'll pop it."

Despite my seeking salvation,
I'm weak in the face of temptation:
I'm hunched with my gin,
Crusted with sin,
Achieving a creamy pulsation

The leader at our local parish
Was a man who was locally cherished…
But now that he's dead,
Some things people said
Indicate habits nightmarish

At music camp, every summer
I got decent at being a drummer...
But when the instructor
Became my abductor,
The next seven years were a bummer

A process poetic and lyrical
Occurs in my flesh-organ spherical:
The juice of creation
Brings multiplication,
So semen is truly a miracle

Each time I pray to the Lord,
My penis is stiff as a board:
I'm praying Louise
Finally gets on her knees,
And sucks on my coital sword

The Limerick,
Restored

A sweet-looking gal, name of Katie,
Was really a devilish lady:
A kiss on her lips
And she'd square up her hips,
To fuck like a demon from Hades

In the schoolhouse down by the farm,
A boy was abused by the marm:
Once done teaching grammar,
She'd force him to slam her,
Causing immeasurable harm

I went to church for a blessing,
But instead, received a caressing:
The priest let me know,
With a tug and a blow,
Desires that he'd been repressing

She sucked on me gently and slowly,
In an act that some say is unholy…
But there's nothing ungodly
'Bout her little body,
Or the way she sucks out my aioli

Predators, all day and night
Don't care if you're loose or you're tight—
They prey on the infirm,
Young teenage interns,
And others unable to fight

Arid, unfucked, and barren,
None ever had fucked Sister Sharon
But her eyes got all wild
When I unzipped and smiled,
Revealing my red-headed baron

The Limerick,
Restored

A disciplined, celibate deacon
Found his defenses were weakened
By the cleavage he'd seen
On a church-going teen,
Who brought on some penile leakin'

My penis is huge, bent, and twisted,
But it's what the good Lord has gifted,
So I do my best
With this dick I was blessed:
With each hump I give her, she's lifted!

The ultimate masculine conquest
Won me a masculine contest:
I bedded a nun
And came on her for fun;
Drenched her in sin with a cum fest

"Casual Day" at my job
Caused our new intern to sob:
Some went to extremes,
Exposing their beans,
And flaunting their vascular throb

I drift toward the blinding white light,
And see such a heavenly sight:
My hot little ex
For celestial sex,
Her pussy eternally tight

SECTION IX:
Drugs & Alcohol

The Limerick,
Restored

A reprobate on cocaine
Had appetites rather untamed:
Once snorting the powder,
He couldn't be louder
Regarding his lust for a dame

A geezer spent all his pension
On an erotic ascension
Buying drugs psychedelic
For orgies angelic,
With hookers from other dimensions

A very odd local café
Served quite a grim cabernet:
Spiked with some blood,
And digestive mud,
And sweat in their best chardonnay

SECTION IX:
Drugs & Alcohol

Insanely addicted to drugs,
She believed she was crawling with bugs…
But it wasn't crack rock—
Her drug was the cock,
So I soothed her and gave her a plug

When you're tripping on acid and dust,
Some sexual touch is a must
You'll be wading through fractals,
Fucking a dactyl,
Dancing with God as you bust

A happy birthday belated
To you, and on topics related,
I hope that the frosting
Was very exhausting—
I laced it to make you sedated

The Limerick,
Restored

My meth has induced a psychosis
And the whiskey, a liver cirrhosis,
And yet I carry on,
Celebrating with songs,
In spite of the dire prognosis

A woman, addicted to reefer,
Was such a magnificent queefer
That each time she puffed,
She puckered her muff,
Laying a vaginal beefer

Drunk on our absinthe and tonic,
We ended our friendship, platonic…
We haven't wedded,
But now that we've bedded,
Our fucking is constant and chronic

At Oktoberfest, drunk on the weizen,
He was sucked like a Hoover or Dyson…
The juice of his wurst
Came forth in a burst,
With plenty more on the horizon

I injected a drug intravenous—
Got me high, but disabled my penis…
Now my only love
Is the opiate glove
That cradles me like I'm a fetus

What an excellent drug that caffeine is
For adding some pep to my penis…
Now I'm at the beach,
Just pounding her peach,
Not worried about who has seen us

The Limerick,
Restored

We ate Psilocybe cubensis,
And came to a rapid consensus:
This trip-happy meal
Was rather ideal
For fucking her out of her senses

When I am hopelessly drunk,
And my penis is seeking a dunk,
I'll fuck any old slag
If she'll open her bag:
A hippie, a prep, or a punk

We took some lysergic acid…
At first, our senses were placid
But once we were tripping,
There'd be no dicking:
My organ was wormy and flaccid

When I'm drunk to the gills on my booze,
I love to have sex in my shoes:
I put on my high-tops,
Whip out my cyclops,
And then a fine fucking ensues

In addition to cocaine and weed,
There are other addictions I feed…
Like the sweet pussy-pie
(Without it, I'd die),
I eat with insatiable greed

Ecstasy, acid, and weed,
Opium, hash, even speed…
I love them all,
Life is a ball,
Drugs are all that I need

The Limerick,
Restored

When I am drunk on Budweiser,
I stroke out a hot little geyser
Drinking and stroking,
My underwear's soaking,
But pleasure's the common divisor

This pot-headed gal, name of Lana,
Smoked mountains of marijuana…
It seemed that the weed
Always gave her the need—
She'd smoke it, and then she would wanna

When I am blowing some lines,
Everyone's lookin' so fine…
Just one little glance
And it's off with my pants,
Diving straight into the 'gine

A cum-loving whore, flabbergasted
Was shocked by with what she was blasted:
Once covered in goop,
She got trapped in a loop,
For his semen was laced with strong acid

A junkie named Sal had to mope
As soon as he ran of dope…
Then I heard him say,
"I swear I'm not gay,
But I'll suck your dick for some coke."

My desperate addiction to meth
Has me nearing my very last breath…
So one final wank
With my last pipe of crank
Will lighten the weight of my death

The Limerick,
Restored

I hatched a nefarious scheme
For my crush to receive all my cream:
I'd whet her with booze,
So she'd suck out my ooze,
Then pilfer her vaginal seam

When sweetie is amped up on coffee,
I can't keep the little gal off me
She claws at my fly,
To pull out my guy,
Hungrily trying to boff me

SECTION X:
Fantasy/Sci-Fi, Paranormal, Horror, & Outré

The Limerick,
Restored

On the Far Eastern isle of Not
Lived a mystical, magical thot…
Her song, sailors lured
For their ailments cured
With her inter-labial snot

In a graveyard rather crepuscular,
A frat boy, lean and quite muscular,
Ran into a goth,
Shared a few shots,
And watched while another was fuckin 'er

A brutally honest old psychic
Said, "The iron is hot, so let's strike it:
My old crystal sphere
Indicates you're a queer,
And your ass is the place where you'd like it."

A youth who sadly, had sinned,
Had her pregnancy cursed by a djinn:
It was still born,
But it had a horn
In its skull, and for arms it had fins

An old Irish lad named O'Connor
Made out like the ole' family Donner:
He had sexual tastes
That left corpses debased;
As he dined, he would toast in their honor

An oneironaut in his dream
Conjured a gal, young and lean
He'd get no consequence
For what dreamland presents,
Even though she was sixteen

The Limerick,
Restored

A wife, after years of abuse,
Took up a knife, not a noose:
Rather than give in,
She'd spike the pig's gin,
And skin that poltroon like a goose

The soul of a dead rapist bastard
Kept it up in the Ghostly Thereafter:
His grim spectral penis
Assaulting each venus,
And blowing a load from the astral

The age-worn masculine wand
Of a wizard from down by the pond
Seduced a nymphette,
Just to settle a bet,
That he could still bag a young blonde

Taken by alien visitors,
I figured they meant something sinister…
Imagine my joy
When they guzzled my toy,
And made me cum by the integer

There once was a horny young druid
Who lived on a river, polluted…
This necromancer
Soon got the cancer,
Right where his balls produce fluid

A cock, escaped from its trousers,
Speared my auntie's young schnauzer,
Then tapped on the keyboard,
Typing in keywords,
Searching for porn on a browser

The Limerick,
Restored

A birthday down by the coast
Sounds like a fine birthday to most…
Not when ravenous gulls
Pick apart the guests' skulls,
And then dismember the host

When I whack off, I'm sobbing and screaming
For sperm cells that live in my semen:
A million nightly
I do not take lightly,
For *all* are deserving of grieving

A station, far out in space,
Was as lonely as most any place…
With two men on the mission,
Both had an admission:
They wanted to go to home base

A zombie, nude and undead,
Failed to fill me with dread…
Though she was decaying,
She looked fine for laying,
And might give some very good head

A young Martian screamer, named Janet
Was fucked by a small Martian manlet
Despite his small stature,
He had her in rapture,
Cumming from planet to planet

Before me appears a white spirit
Too sexy for me to fear it:
Its titties, so ghostly,
Harden me mostly;
I'm stroking whenever I'm near it

The Limerick,
Restored

A witch's big tits made a goblin
Get thick, and veiny, and throbbin'…
So grinning a grin,
The goblin dove in,
Pounding the witch's red robin

The ancient one, wise and sooth,
Granted a kernel of truth:
"Two knuckles deep,
Past the brink you must seek,
To promise a powerful boof."

When I dream, I often imagine,
I'm slaying a cum-breathing dragon:
I save the girl,
She sucks on my pearls,
We flee in a wiener-drawn wagon

In the far reaches of space,
A big-titted alien race
Came onboard my craft
To tit-fuck my shaft,
And jiggle all over the place

Have you ever been fucked by a demon?
This hellspawn was having me creamin'…
I shall not embellish:
The sex was quite hellish,
But drained me of all of my semen

A corpse with no life in its brain
Was freed from its deathly domain:
The doc brought his wife
Half-back to life,
To cum in her soulless remains

The Limerick,
Restored

There's a creature that lives in the ducts,
And emerges at night for a suck
Its lips are so fast,
I instantly blast
Its throat full of seminal muck

I prowl, at night after dark,
Hunting my prey like a shark,
But luckily, my bite
Is surprisingly light
When I hump your dog in the park

I'm away on a magical trip,
On a magical, sexual ship,
Looking for hotties
With magical bodies
To suck on their magical nips

Bigfoot, a lusty old ape,
Leaves many campers agape...
If you're wowed by his feet,
You're in for a treat;
His cock's a gargantuan shape

There once was a nasty old troll
With an ogreish, vile old soul
Hiding up in the hills,
For sexual thrills,
Abusing a gnome's little hole

Hung like a horse was my teacher,
A muscled and marvelous creature:
My sexual mentor,
He was a centaur,
His cock his most excellent feature

The Limerick,
Restored

I'm a pervy, predator ass-man,
Prowling the sexual grassland…
To get a gazelle,
Give 'er booty a smell—
To catch em' I have to run fast, man

She's perched in the tree like a hawk,
For prey she will silently stalk…
Her eyes see them all,
No matter how small,
Scanning the meadow for cock

At the séance, my dead grandma said,
"We're bored in the land of the dead.
So my friends come along
When you diddle your dong;
We watch you jerking in bed."

A being emerged from a mound,
Looking for something to pound…
It feeds in the night,
Fucking anything tight,
Then scurries back into the ground

Last night, had a hell of a time
Getting blowjobs and doing some lines…
But some newspaper pics
Of who sucked my dick
Said she died in July '99

When I delivered to house 104,
Said the woman who stood by the door:
"This morning at six,
I was sucking your dick!"
— But I'd never seen her before

The Limerick,
Restored

When she denies me a ride,
I poison the bitch with some cyanide…
When she's just north of dead,
I can get her in bed,
And easily then get my guy inside

There once was a girl named Esther,
Who lived on the bad side of Chester
Down by the tracks,
She was tossed in a sack
So a vagrant gang could molest her

I'd prefer that there be no witness
(After all, it's nobody's business),
But while I was jerking,
Someone was lurking,
Scaring me totally shitless

A sexual vampire-ghost
Attached to the cock of its host…
It sucked out his soul
From the small, puckered hole
On top of his virile post

After a chemical spill,
I became violently ill:
I felt nearly dead,
My cock grew two heads,
And I developed some gills

More or less, it's all in plain sight,
The kids at his house late at night…
His sexual violence
Relies on our silence
To never be brought to the light

The Limerick,
Restored

A naked creature is prowling,
Hiding in bedrooms and growling…
This *thing* in my house
Is my sex-crazy spouse,
So desperate to fuck that she's howling

I climbed over your white picket fences
To fuck you right out of your senses…
I wasn't sure what you meant
When you didn't consent,
So now I've been charged with offenses

A very well-hung creature crept
Into my bed while I slept
I never sleep tight,
'Cause it's here every night;
It's something I've come to accept

SECTION X:
Fantasy/Sci-Fi, Paranormal, Horror, & Outré

They burst in, and knocked out my son,
But the horror had only begun:
After they burglarized,
My wife was pulverized,
And filled with their horrible cum

With my camera, I sit in my car
To film my young video stars…
It has been ruled
I can't go near a school,
But I still tape the kids from afar

A pointy-eared virginoid halfling
Sought his first gash for the mashing:
A forest nymphette
Received his pipette,
Delightedly moaning and thrashing

The Limerick,
Restored

A lurker appears in my yard,
Jerking incredibly hard…
Standing where he can see
My young daughter pee,
And now she's incredibly scarred

This bitch is as dark as they come,
With kinks that most people would shun…
What sick person yearns
To be stuffed full of worms,
Wriggling out of their bum?

Convinced that I'd seek pussy tighter,
She attacked with a switchblade and lighter…
With my lover unhinged,
My pubes were all singed,
For I was too frightened to fight her

I've been having these nightmarish dreams,
Where nothing is quite as it seems…
My penis squirts blood,
Which comes in a flood,
Instead of my seminal cream

Cooped up in the nuclear shelter,
While she was sleeping, I felt her…
Then I gave her a baste, and
Was kicked to the wasteland,
To live with the mutants and swelter

Bereft by the loss of our leader,
Someone else must impregnate our breeder:
To build a foundation
For repopulation,
We need a new alpha to seed her

The Limerick,
Restored

The demigod hoots and he chortles
As he enters her dry anal portal…
This wicked archangel
Likes sex to be painful
Whenever he's fucking a mortal

When children are spritely and little,
I lure them with chocolate and Skittles…
Once they're in my van,
Next up in my plan,
Is giving their privates a diddle

The fun of exotic gastronomy
Mixed with the thrill of astronomy
When she tasted the sperm
Of an alien worm
From an unearthly ecology

SECTION X:
Fantasy/Sci-Fi, Paranormal, Horror, & Outré

People quite friendly and formal,
In private, might not be as normal:
Though during the week
They're typical geeks,
They're living a nightmare nocturnal

I killed dozens of hookers with glee
On my sexual murdering spree…
But they used DNA
To put me away,
And now I will never be free

You can hear my nasally breathing,
And within me, my semen is seething…
I'm covered in grease
As I get my release
Behind Wendy's, late in the evening

SECTION XI:
BDSM

The Limerick,
Restored

A gal's fantasies about rape
Left her booty-hole always agape…
'Twas easy to enter,
'Till she found a mentor
Who kept it shut up with some tape

Her body was quite mediocre
But still, I wanted to poke her:
She said I was hot
And she liked me a lot,
And she'd love if I'd paddle and choke her

A gal on the verge of divorce
Craved being used with some force…
Her husband, vanilla,
Couldn't fuck, the poor fella,
Despite being hung like a horse

SECTION XI:
BDSM

A paddle, cut out of cedar,
He used whenever he'd beat 'er…
Her penchant for pain
Had her craving the grain
Of the paddle as Master would seed 'er

A masochist, itching for pain,
Took it to levels insane…
From bees in her cunt,
And other such stunts,
Like needles stuck into her brain

The ageplayer Betty Dupree
Practiced the Dd/lg…
This "daughter" would grin
Before he'd stick it in
And say "No daddy, I'm only three!"

The Limerick,
Restored

A little, whiny and hyper,
Liked to poop into her diaper...
Her 24/7,
His punishments heaven,
Spanked her so hard as he wiped her

She told me, honest and firm,
That I'm only a sub-human worm...
It's true that I'm dirt,
Barely good for a squirt—
A fact my Mistress confirmed

A sub, property of his owner,
Was permitted to be a big stoner
In fact, his Domme
Like to insert his bong
Up his ass 'till it gave him a boner

For a masochist versed in his practice,
There comes escalation in tactics…
This is why, just last week,
He tried something unique,
And fucked himself dry with a cactus

Ass plugs are my pleasure and joy,
A thrilling and all-filling toy
But since I met a "feeder,"
My plug's an impeder,
Preventing two pounds of bok choi…

By God, there are children to raise,
Lunches and beds to be made…
And for a prosperous life,
A subservient wife
Ought to worship her man's mayonnaise

The Limerick,
Restored

A pathetic, shriveled-dick cuck
Had to watch his hot wifey get fucked
By a bevy of Bulls,
So there'd be no lulls
In all of the cocks she would suck

Littles like stuffies and blankies, and
Being bratty to earn lots of spankies…
Because Daddy's demands
Are enforced with his hands,
Or paddles when baby is cranky

A husband was quite fond of sharing,
Just as fond was he for staring:
While his wifey was gored,
He never got bored,
And the Bull adored all his glaring

When you're roleplaying with non-consent,
You can roleplay one hundred percent:
The safe word's "chateau,"
So that she can scream "No,"
And the fucking still will not relent

When she's in the midst of a lay,
She craves a dark sexual play:
A really hard choke,
Or a smack from her bloke,
And her worries will all melt away

I once knew a sub, name of Maddie,
A floppy and jiggling fattie…
Her gargantuan size
Might turn off other guys,
But flab is so sexy to Daddy

The Limerick,
Restored

When you have a slave, you can lend
Her holes to be used by a friend:
I called up my buddy,
To fill her with putty,
Right in her little rear end

The sadist had found a cum dumpster
Who'd let him slap her and thump her…
But he found out too late
He'd be jailed by eight:
Turned out that the slut was a youngster

She knows what her body is for:
To be used and abused like a whore
So for men who are raving,
She's happily slaving,
Chained and spread wide on the floor

If you date a girl who's poor,
You can treat her like she's just a whore
And if she is rich,
Treat her just like a bitch,
And then you can give 'er your spore

Oh, what magnificent luck
That her hubby's a feminized schmuck:
She domineers
By dressing him queer;
A sissy for Mistress to cuck

While I am down in my dungeon,
My penis is constantly lunging…
After it grows,
Forward it goes,
Into the subs I am plunging

The Limerick,
Restored

This girl asked me to choke her,
But I did it so hard that I broke her:
A vocal cord tear
Had her gasping for air,
And now, the gal is a croaker

Her paypig, a sissy named Frank,
Gave her the reigns to his bank…
She spent his last dollar,
So he lives in squalor,
But she can still give him a spank

My submissive, obedient bae
Always does what I say…
And if she refuses,
I paint her with bruises,
And whip 'er to shit during play

SECTION XI:
BDSM

If she's into bondage, perhaps,
You can restrain her with straps
Then put clamps on her nips,
And brandish a whip,
And punish that hot little snack

I worship the ground where she stands,
For I'm an inferior man…
SissyMeet.com
Is where I met my Domme,
And I bow to her every demand

Forgive me as I reminisce
'Bout a sub, whom I quite dearly miss…
When you own a toilet,
You've got to soil it,
And this one would guzzle my piss

The Limerick,
Restored

I simply tug on your leash
Whenever I need a release...
That's how you know
It's time to come blow,
And eagerly pleasure my piece

Violence, when it's consensual,
Can be surprisingly sensual:
Lovingly smack a bitch,
Use her to fap a bit—
Orgasm will be eventual

She was underwhelmed by his stuff,
But never asked for it rough...
So poor, gentle Mike
Didn't know what she liked,
And worried he wasn't enough

For the boss of a big corporation,
Submission brings total elation:
It's a sweet, freeing joy
To become someone's toy
At the end of a day of frustration

When I whip my sub with a wire,
It burns on her skin like a fire…
But don't feel pity
For her stinging titties,
For pain is her primal desire

A gal with a boyfriend, milquetoast
Proposed a gangbang spit-roast…
She told him "Don't worry,
I'll cum from a flurry
Of cocks, maybe seven at most."

The Limerick,
Restored

A vampiric Master named Brad
Took every orgasm I had…
Now I can't cum,
Though I fuck everyone;
Empty, lonely, and sad

When it comes to lecherous acts,
Here is an obvious fact:
Sexually savage,
Women want to be ravaged:
Tied, and pounded, and slapped

I once knew a damn dirty Brit
Who enjoyed being covered in spit…
But for acts more degrading,
She took some persuading,
Before she'd agree to submit

My penis, the size of a club,
Is always in search of a rub
Too big for insertion,
I opt for coercion,
Or maybe a size-queening sub

One ex I especially miss
Could plant an exceptional kiss…
But what I miss most of all
Is the way she would crawl
'Tween my legs to be drenched in my piss

This is the only demand
For the ladies, madams and ma'ams:
You're just playthings and toys
For enjoyment of boys,
To pleasure our sexual glands

The Limerick,
Restored

Boys, you'd better take note:
You're nothing but dick and some scrote
You're disposable meat
For the ladies to eat;
An object for women to tote

For many, running away
Makes for the kinkiest play:
The pursuit and the catch
Will earn you the snatch
After you capture your prey

In bed, the gal indicated,
She liked feeling that she was hated…
So as I was thrusting,
Told her she was disgusting,
So that she would feel degraded

SECTION XI:
BDSM

The furious force of my slammage
Put her at a keen disadvantage:
Poor little Sally,
I ruined her valley, and
Caused irreversible damage

SECTION XII:
Sexual & Anatomical Obsessions

The Limerick,
Restored

Men, creatures simple and lusty,
Can be tricked by most any old hussie:
We'll do what you say
When your twins come to play,
So do let them breathe if you're busty

For us men who appreciate breasts,
It's not always big we like best:
Small, puffy, or saggy,
We'll worship the baggies,
Regardless of what's on your chest

A man fond of fucking balloons,
Had crates full of rubber and lube
He'd fill them all night,
Pushing with might,
And pop them whenever he spewed

I'm a bitch with a sickening mind—
Any rod or pole is a sign:
If it's narrow or long,
Or resembles a dong,
My panties are flooded with slime

I once knew a husband—a cheat,
Who followed the whims of his meats:
Each time he was out,
He'd lose it, the lout,
Upon seeing feminine teats

Entranced by hard nipples and vanity,
A man ceased to see the humanity
In pieces of tail
He so longed to rail,
In fits of lustful insanity

The Limerick,
Restored

A boor, who shall remain nameless,
Was known for impulses quite tameless:
He'd pinch all the tushes,
Then jump in the bushes;
Persistent, sneaky, and shameless

The summery secret of lasses,
Eyes hidden by mirrored sunglasses:
They're sneaking a stare
At all our affairs;
Our abs, our arms, and our asses

A phallus, veiny and eager
To submerge to its nuts into beaver,
Has only one use:
To thrust 'till the juice
Erupts in a passionate fever

A boy had his soundness assessed
Due to urges he sadly possessed:
He'd grope and he'd claw
To expose what he saw;
Completely obsessed with the breast

The unfortunate fact for one man
Was that sex came from only his hand…
The bliss from his kink
Was gone in a blink,
And it shriveled the life from his gland

Every half, full, and new moon,
My gal would become quite the loon:
She'd demand to be choked,
'Till the sheets were so soaked
That soon we lived in a lagoon

The Limerick,
Restored

When a girl gives you The Eyes,
You know she will give you The Prize…
All you must do
Is give her a screw,
And pleasure The Thing in her thighs

A crotch with some fur is a plus,
For it shows that you're not one to fuss…
Plus it tickles my chin
When I come in
To lick on your peppery puss

The first of all masculine tests
Is how a man handles a breast:
Is he gentle or rough?
Does he suck it enough?
Does he pull it, or keep it compressed?

I joined a support club, fraternal
For sex addicts, sick and nocturnal
Late at night with the urging,
We whack off to purge it,
And write it all down in a journal

I've noticed your big, pouty lips...
How an infant might fit in your hips...
But nothing distracts
As when titties are packed
Into sports bras with powerful nips

I tried to stuff meat tortellini,
But chef was too much of a meanie...
He wouldn't take
A stuffing of steak
With meat if it came from my weenie

The Limerick,
Restored

The sex menu was table d'hôte:
One ass, one pussy, one throat…
Choose brunette or a blond,
Or if you are fond,
A gal with a mammary bloat

I like watching creatures, aquatic—
Their motions are more than hypnotic
Those tentacles reaching,
And whale holes breaching…
I find it all very erotic

When tight little Kelly bent over,
Her ass formed the shape of a clover…
One horny guy
Took a look at her thighs,
And what he did next was he drove her

This manwhore I know was an urbanite
Who bagged more bitches than Dolomite
He's moved out of the city,
But still craves the pretties,
So now he's a slutty suburbanite

The problem with being a flirt
Is the boys will be desperate to squirt…
I hope you like dairy,
'Cause inside our berries,
Our glands make a powerful 'gurt

So hungry were my horny ways,
That I fucked the whole réchauffé
Voracious and hasty,
I plunged the puff pastry,
And then came inside the entrée

The Limerick,
Restored

I'm a lover of sex and cuisine…
An eating and fucking machine!
Unzip and unbutton,
I'll give you my mutton,
And sample your feminine bean

I slunk off with a gal, name of Donna
To feed her a snack in the sauna…
For this cum-loving tart,
The very best part
Was tasting testicular fauna

I get a spasmodic squirt
When a tittie hangs out of a shirt…
The sight of that boob,
It hardens my tube,
As my admiral stands at alert

Hard-working balls never tire:
Once full, they're desperate to fire
So just clench your cheeks
To hold in the leaks,
And manage your carnal desire

When feminine nipples are hardened,
It awakens my masculine garden
It'll be just a jiffy
'Fore I get a stiffie,
And may have to ask for your pardon

During her sexual moods,
Her mouth took a turn for the lewd…
Upping the stakes
With the cocks that she takes,
She sucked on her fiftieth dude

The Limerick,
Restored

My leathery genital dermis
Burns as hot as a furnace…
And all of this heat
Trapped in my meat
Leads me to acts of impureness

My tender, masculine beans
Are always alive in my jeans…
Ready for jerking,
They're always working
Producing ancestral proteins

The thought of my organ most private
Is "If there is a hole, I will drive it!"
But this hussy, McKenzie
Put me into a frenzy
So much that she didn't survive it

SECTION XII:
Sexual & Anatomical Obsessions

When a an outfit reveals the fracture
Between breasts, or the vaginal pasture,
My balls lift up high,
Confirming supply
Of semen my balls manufacture

I'm addicted to fucking like crazy,
But often am feeling quite lazy
So she lowers her socket,
My cock primed to rock it,
And gyrates her feminine daisy

It can be terribly tiring
For balls to always be firing,
For it is exhausting
To force out your frosting
From morning until you're retiring

The Limerick,
Restored

There's much more to falling in love
Than courtship, snuggles, and doves…
There's still the issue
Of erectile tissue,
And stuffing the vaginal glove

When I fuck, I make it high-risk,
Which means that one must be brisk:
Just a quickie with Sally,
Down in the alley,
To give her my seminal bisque

The sensation of all my blood flowing
Into my cock as it's growing
Is heavenly bliss
Combined with a kiss,
Right where the precum is showing

As a man, I can strictly affirm,
There's nothing as pretty as sperm:
The gel of my testicles,
Soaring majestical,
Out of my penile worm

Her body was so taught and lean,
Yet her parts were as plump as I'd seen:
Her ass, so developed,
I'd like to envelop
My cock though the cheeks in between

When a girl is looking to bang,
She'll be watching your crotch—how it hangs
If she notices meat,
You're in for a treat,
As long as she doesn't have fangs

The Limerick,
Restored

The first breast that I'd ever feel
Was a thrill that was almost surreal…
Next thing I knew,
I was desperate to screw,
And I fucked with remarkable zeal

My penis, the size of a cashew,
Is searching for gashes to mash through…
But ladies just laugh
At the size of my staff,
And now my self-doubt, I must hash through

I'm into this girl named Laura,
Who just has the sexiest aura…
And I get so stiff
When I get a whiff
Of all her vaginal flora

Right in the back of my car
Is my personal favorite, by far
Of places to dash
For a mid-workday smash,
And fuck someone full of my tar

I once knew a gal, name of Sadie
Whose dealings were sexually shady:
A new man she would seek
For each day of the week,
Which is conduct unfit for a lady

This ravenous girl I dated
Kept me forever fellated:
No matter how much she'd chug,
She'd need more, like a drug,
And was never entirely sated

The Limerick,
Restored

A teenager, tight and unsullied,
Not once had a cock in her gully…
But soon she would get
So unbearably wet,
She'd end up fucking her bully

Ejaculate, ever so buttery,
Inspires all manner of sluttery:
I did a bukkake
One night in Milwaukee;
She bathed in our penile nuttery

I'm mesmerized and entranced
By that jiggling, wiggling dance:
No bra for the breasts
Is what works the best
To harden the thing in my pants

SECTION XII:
Sexual & Anatomical Obsessions

I often find myself craving
The suck of a sexual maven…
One who will lend
My penile friend
An orgasmically warm little haven

Don't waste any money on lace,
Or a bigger TV for your place
His needs aren't complex—
He just wants your sex,
And to hump on your glorious face

Forgive me for being obsessive
Over breasts I find quite impressive…
Even when I'm not attracted,
I'm still distracted
By tits with dimensions excessive

The Limerick,
Restored

I'm really feeling the heat,
Tryn'a fuck every gal that I meet:
First, I seduce,
Then I give her my juice,
Then I dump her back into the street

I suddenly see with great clarity
The depth of my carnal barbarity
I'm just a fuck monkey,
Shooting my spunky,
And basking in filth and vulgarity

Have you ever dated a squirmer?
She'll sit on your seminal wormer
Then wiggle, psychotic,
In fits so erotic,
It milks all the goo from your spermer

She knew she'd finally get hired
If she wore more revealing attire…
But then wasn't respected,
Though some were erected,
Engorged with the blood of desire

Will my unending lust ever fade?
The answer is no, I'm afraid…
My utter fixation
On hot fornication
Will never be fully allayed

A virgin, unfucked and so pure,
Is blessed with a certain allure…
But I get bigger thrills
Fucking someone with skills;
Sexually adept and mature

The Limerick,
Restored

I once knew a curvy young lassy,
Delightfully sexy and sassy
She had attitude,
And looked great in the nude:
Busty, supple, and assy

One summer, a girl named Wanda
Craved the man-anaconda
She took daily snake
Down by the lake,
And at night, in the back of her Honda

My longing for love is so great,
But I'm mired in endless self-hate…
Since I'm mentally sick
'Bout the size of my dick,
I'll never find love in a mate

SECTION XII:
Sexual & Anatomical Obsessions

Nubiles, so taut and young,
Are plenty of sexual fun
But when I jam my Luger
Into a cougar,
The cream really shoots from my gun

Through farms and fields I frolic,
Fucking the bitches, bucolic
And when they make me splatter,
All of my batter
Ejects in an arc, parabolic

Have you ever slept with a swinger?
She'll put your dick through the ringer
Since she fucks all the time,
It'll boggle your mind
How much will come out of your flinger

The Limerick,
Restored

For me, there is nothing as neat
As the inter-labial treat:
As soon as I see
That wet little pea,
The blood'll flow straight to my meat

I spent all the last of my cash
On hookers I happily mashed...
But now that I'm broke,
I'm a lonely old bloke
With an incurable rash

Go find a girl who knows
The way to administer blows:
A tongue on the top,
Where the cum will soon pop,
Produces the seminal flows

SECTION XII:
Sexual & Anatomical Obsessions

My penis is so chafed and sore
From slam-bangin' all of these whores…
My wiener is tired,
But more I will hire:
Still, I crave many more

When horny, I find myself perving
On women who are not deserving…
When I've a hard bone,
I can't leave them alone,
My presence acutely unnerving

My crush was attracted to beards,
So I had one next time I appeared…
I grew it in thick,
And powdered my dick,
But the beard-loving bitch disappeared

The Limerick,
Restored

Women, once they are wet,
Are perverted as any you've met:
They go into a craze
When their pussy's ablaze,
Desperate to ride your baguette

A moth is drawn to a flame,
And me, I'm mostly the same:
When I catch a glimpse
Of those mammary blimps,
I wander straight toward the dame

In a fit of invention quite manic,
I invented a gizmo, ceramic
My blood it reroutes
To my masculine spout,
For purposes hemodynamic

SECTION XII:
Sexual & Anatomical Obsessions

Sometimes, it just feels easy
To live my life nasty and sleazy
So the life that I lead
Is filthy indeed,
And might make you feel uneasy

A girl, I swear it to Jesus,
Used to get off with hard cheeses
When her building got rats,
There was no more of that,
For fear of their rodent diseases

They say that I am a loner
Alone, just holding my boner
But I know a gal
Who's a very close pal,
And also one hell of a moaner

The Limerick,
Restored

When our penises are well-received,
We are so very relieved,
For fear that our stuff
Just won't be enough
To leave our gal pleasantly pleased

Her pussy, completely exceptional,
Would fuck you from every directional...
From left to the right,
She always stayed tight,
With movements extremely effectual

Tiny, tight little dresses
Are adding to all of my stresses:
When they hike up their skirt,
I suddenly squirt,
Leaving behind little messes

SECTION XII:
Sexual & Anatomical Obsessions

Reviewing my cash and expenses,
I'm seeing some cash consequences
Due to my spending
On hookers unending,
To fuck me right out of my senses

I apologize if my eyes wander
To the bosom that's hidden down yonder…
Your tits make me dream
Of shooting my cream
On blouses you'll then have to launder

Oh, how absurd is the sex,
With its oozing and slippery mess…
Its farts and its drool,
Hairy nuts and the grool,
The flopping and slapping of flesh!

The Limerick,
Restored

If you want to stay quite fit and lean,
Work out on the reg, and eat clean
For the best exercise,
You should fuck lots of guys,
Becoming a fucking machine

When titties are hidden away,
It saddens the brightest of days…
But show me the crest
On the curve of your breast,
And it sets my penis ablaze

She slurps with such obvious greed,
Frantic to get at my seed
It's her favorite snack,
Which explains her attack,
When she is desperate to feed

As a farmer, I'd sure like to slam
My beef in your tight little lamb
My corn cob needs shucking,
So on with the fucking—
I'm desperate to harvest your yam

Pregnant, milk-leaking udders
Make me a very big nutter:
The way the tits swell
Makes me horny as hell,
When maidens are turned into mothers

Forgive me if this appears crass,
But I am obsessed with your ass…
The way that the seat
Curves into your meat
Is making me harder than glass

The Limerick,
Restored

The way that gals stared at my abs
Was rather arousing and fab…
But now that I'm older,
And slouching my shoulders,
My muscles are covered in flab

It is a fact, undeniable
That my semen is potent and viable…
I'm rearing and fertile,
So come get a squirtle
If you like your semen reliable

When licked by a man in moustache,
This floozie will cum in a flash
The way that your whisker
Tickles her pisser
Will cause her to quiver and thrash

SECTION XII:
Sexual & Anatomical Obsessions

Obligations I am all shirking,
For I prefer to be lurking:
In halls and libraries,
My habit is scary,
Watching and stroking my gerkin

She's never fully disrobed,
For nudity's something she loathes
That's why all her skirts
Are stained with my squirts:
She prefers that the fucking is clothed

So horny was my gal Gail,
She left behind her a trail:
Because of the path
From the ooze of her snatch,
She's often mistook for a snail

The Limerick,
Restored

Does it make me a pervert or wretch
If I like to watch girls stretch?
It hardens my lance—
If you look at my pants,
You'll see a cock outline is etched

There is a technique I'm espousing
To please my penile housing:
When ready to sin,
Lick under the skin;
A technique my glans finds arousing

Have you ever told an untruth
To access the vaginal booth?
Sometimes, guys are lyin'
When they are tryin'
To fuck a Vanessa or Ruth

Late nights, I'm hard at work sewing
Some trousers designed for the blowing:
There's a hole in the front
For your penis or cunt—
It's open, so everything's showing

The best thing about knowing a moper
Is whenever you want, you can grope her
Since she's already sad,
She won't get mad,
And might even smoke on your poker

This is a fact you can quote:
Gus was obsessed with the throat
In your esophagus,
You will suck off a Gus;
He loves the tunnel you tote

The Limerick,
Restored

Along with her other afflictions,
She had a penis addiction…
She was deaf, dumb, and blind,
And out of her mind,
But fucked with impressive conviction

When she is so skinny and thin,
I can't ram it when I stick it in
A well-padded thrust
Really pleases my lust,
And makes for more pleasurable sin

Every time my dick has the wood,
I think, "There's a hole that I could… "
But just 'cause you *could*,
Doesn't mean that you *should*,
'Cause not every hole is so good

SECTION XII:
Sexual & Anatomical Obsessions

When I see her, my boner's a riser,
Eager to weasel inside 'er...
At inopportune times,
It pumps up and climbs;
A stubborn and stiff fertilizer

I've had quite the sexual lull,
And now my balls are too full...
So any gal sighting
Is quickly igniting
My hardened erectile bull

Her goat milker, opened for thou,
Is perfect to plunge and to plough
So I say, take her up,
And plunge with your pup,
As often as she will allow

The Limerick,
Restored

A hooker or two I will greet
When I need to empty my meat...
Like that fake-titted bimbo,
Standing akimbo,
Bathing in red neon heat

Even a dumb, simple layman
Knows how to plunge a foramen:
Penile admission
Is pure intuition,
When you're equipped with a stamen

I enter into a fever
As soon as she touches my lever...
She's rubbing it stiff
So it's hard in a jiff,
Ready to enter her beaver

When I'm looking for something to drink,
I turn to the fountain of pink
From there, I will dredge
The vaginal wedge
To suck out the feminine ink

Go and lie flat on your back—
My cock needs a hot little snack!
Now prepare to receive
My dick in your sheath,
As I pummel your vaginal crack

Her fluttering cunt does a dance
Which inspires an oral romance
She is so graceful
When she gives me a faceful,
And I'm in a cunt-eating trance

The Limerick,
Restored

A sophisticated gourmet
Really knows how to savor a lay:
Drizzle oil from truffles
On her mammary duffles,
And pair with a fine cabernet

One thrust from my meaty bolete
Can put any bitch into heat:
My beefy porcini,
A glorious weenie,
Will knock her right off of her feet

The sexist thing about backs
Is how they lead down to the crack…
So when I see it bare,
My cum I will share,
Proceeding to empty my sack

SECTION XII:
Sexual & Anatomical Obsessions

She's wild and licking her lip,
And it's causing a seminal drip:
When she gives me The Eyes,
I point to her thighs,
And give her a seminal dip

Since she's extremely adorable,
I have thoughts rather deplorable
It must be her hips,
Or her ever-hard nips
That make her look perfectly gore-able

Gals'r honored when I bequeath
My glorious, vascular beef:
As I insert it,
The trapped air is squirted,
And out comes a glorious queef

The Limerick,
Restored

When I noticed her strong, juicy legs,
I wanted to knock up her eggs
So I said "Hi, I'm Steve…
Now would you receive
The seed from my virile peg?"

I have such excessive free time,
That I live a lifestyle divine:
My only work
Is the pump and the jerk,
The squirting and splattering slime

Hey, meat might be murder,
But at least my meat is a squirter
And when I'm rock-hard,
My cum will shoot far,
As long as I'm stiff as a girder

I have interests in things rather groovy,
Like surfing and comics and movies,
But more than them all,
I'm deeply enthralled
By pairs of jiggling boobies

Her body, firm and so taut,
Was getting my cock really hot…
Tried to get her to blow me,
But first she must know me—
Turns out that she isn't a thot

He's a simpleton, dolt, and a brute,
But the gals get so wet for his glutes…
Turns out a great butt
Turns them all into sluts,
Even if you've the brains of a newt

The Limerick,
Restored

Because I'm a horny young male,
I have a stiff frontal tail…
I'm quick to the bust,
So sex is a must,
I only need someone to nail

Unmarried and already 30,
She knew it was time to get dirty:
Her biological clock
Made her desperate for cock,
To impregnate her tight little birdie

Each morning, if only I could,
I'd show you my big morning wood,
So you could admire
My penile fire,
And tell me it looks very good

SECTION XII:
Sexual & Anatomical Obsessions

Sunday, my one day of rest,
I get snuggled up in my nest:
My dick in my hand,
A squirt from my gland…
Jerking all day is the best

Just like a warm summer breeze,
I enter her pussy with ease…
Under her gown,
The hole that I pound
Is perfect to pump full of cheese

Her orgasm comes in a moan
It's the prettiest music I've known...
Like a voice violin
Of pleasure and sin,
That hits such a marvelous tone

The Limerick,
Restored

For cum lovers, soon after meeting,
Begins the feverish feeding:
They're hungry to chug
Your seminal drug
To get all the semen they're needing

I think it is ever-so dandy
To suck on your vaginal candy:
Your feminine skittle,
So sweaty and little,
Is sweeter than brittle or shandy

I'm an emotional guy,
And prove it with tears that I cry…
So when I see your bootie,
The wondrous beauty
Might bring a tear to my eye

Women like romance and candles,
Not guys wearing cargos and sandals...
They like men who dress fine,
And appreciate wine,
And will fuck their sweet pussies to shambles

He spent hours on calculations
To solve for the perfect gyration...
But despite his math genius
He was lame with his penis,
And subject to sudden deflation

My sexy and beautiful sweetie
Gets just a little bit needy:
Two days without dick
And she's practically sick,
Desperate to suck something meaty

The Limerick,
Restored

In her tiny tube top with no bra,
Her body had nary-a flaw:
This little tart, Audrey
Was lookin' quite tawdry…
The sluttiest I ever saw

Masturbation addiction
Is not such an awful affliction…
After all, nothing's wrong
With stroking your schlong
To cum from the rhythm and friction

As soon as my boner has risen,
It just wants to snuggle a pigeon…
A warm little birdie
To get me so dirty,
And help me to cum just a smidgen

SECTION XII:
Sexual & Anatomical Obsessions

A pussy's a semen extractor,
Depending on numerous factors:
For one, is it tight?
Is it gripping me right?
Is she cumming, or is she an actor?

I am the boobie inspector,
Here to suck out your nectar...
If there is lactation,
Come down to the station,
And I will insert my injector

My favorite sexual treat
Is a pair of beautiful feet...
My cock really grows
For those wiggling toes;
The blood will flow straight to my meat

The Limerick,
Restored

I have a hole in my chest
From losing the gal I love best...
So sexy and smart,
With talents in art,
And pointy, magnificent breasts

White, Asian, or black,
I go wild when I see a rack...
With titties revealed,
My fate becomes sealed:
I've gotta sneak off for a whack

They can all see my raging wood,
So they know that I've got something good...
When I'm hard in the sauna,
They know that they wanna,
But they aren't so sure if they should

I'm quite a kinky young fella,
Anything but vanilla…
I'll fuck you with dowels,
And gardening trowels,
And even a jumbo umbrella

Aside from my interests scholastic,
I'm also a fan of gymnastics…
Those form-fitting tights
Make for wonderful sights:
The bulges and butts are fantastic

I have a female companion
With quite a delectable canyon…
When I get a taste,
She's sure to be braced—
I'll gobble with reckless abandon

The Limerick,
Restored

Had no condoms, but I didn't care,
'Cause she had such a jiggly pair...
So she got on her knees
But I had a disease,
And gave her a medical scare

I'm a totally miserable mess,
Completely fucking depressed:
Since my sweetie-pie dumped me,
She'll no longer hump me...
Her pussy was simply the best

I once knew a girl named Marge
Who treasured the thrill of my discharge:
When she gets it shooting,
She's cheering and hooting;
Excited by cum from a dick large

SECTION XII:
Sexual & Anatomical Obsessions

Once I give the titties a squeeze,
I slide into their slimebox with ease...
I just have to hope
They like being groped,
Or I will be forced to appease

I'm desperately gloomy and lonely,
For I've nobody to bone me...
So I stick my sad rocket
Into a pocket:
A jumbo cheese ravioli

Once my penis is in it,
It doesn't last more than a minute...
My sexing is fast
'Cause I'm quick to the blast—
If it were a race, I would win it

The Limerick,
Restored

She likes fishin', muddin', and mullets,
And redneck cock in her gullet:
If you are a hick,
She'll suck on your dick,
Whether you've got a cannon or bullet

When I'm scorching with lust and desire,
I sizzle and drip and perspire...
I thrust and I grunt
With a feverous shunt,
Delivering seminal fire

Oh, what a curious curse
To have such a hot little nurse...
While she tends to my wounds,
I grope her balloons,
And diddle her vaginal purse

SECTION XII:
Sexual & Anatomical Obsessions

As soon as I saw her in lace,
I splooged all over the place:
Her butt, her hair,
Her titties so fair,
And even her beautiful face

When I'm hard in my area private,
I yearn for a girl to ride it...
Stiff as concrete,
My powerful meat
Is eager, so do not deprive it

When it comes to mammary tissue,
My obsession is sometimes an issue...
If groping can start,
But then you depart,
I will so desperately miss you

The Limerick,
Restored

The Male Imagination
For jiggles, twerks, and gyration
Can be so realistic—
Although we're simplistic,
We have very vivid fixations

When she has gigantomastia,
My thoughts just couldn't get nastia…
I like tits so vast,
They throw out her back,
And give her a case of sleep apnea

The great thing about mouths, it is true,
They can do things a pussy can't do:
The tongue and the lips
Are a treat for our dicks,
Erupting in marvelous goo

I wasn't even remotely attracted,
But my penis just gets so distracted…
She is ugly, although
She's quick to the blow,
So semen would still be extracted

While exciting her feminine yolk,
Her labia soon will be soaked…
These are the signs
That you've readied her 'gine
For a vigorous penile poke

A gal, quite beyond post-pubescence
Had an ass shaped like billowy crescents
Even younger men knew
She'd be eager to screw,
And their lust turned out to be prescient

The Limerick,
Restored

A horny young lass, name of Shalyn
Was known for her squirming and flailin'...
One evening in bed,
She fucked a gent dead,
And now behind bars she is wailin'

The deep-throating game, you shall win
Once your scrotum can rest on her chin:
She'll breathe through her nose
As she swallows your hose,
With slapping from both of your skin

It's a difficult thing, when you're broke,
To find a gal as a bloke...
But you still have a chance
To get in their pants
As long as you're hung like an oak

SECTION XII:
Sexual & Anatomical Obsessions

A gal's sartorial style
Aroused my organ, penile…
Her shirt was so low,
Her tits were exposed;
My wiener grew by a mile

As humans, we're rather complex,
But as mammals, we simply need sex:
Spermatic induction
Allows reproduction,
So humping is what we do best

She loved how he was so kind,
And polite, of intelligent mind,
And how back at her house,
He ripped off her blouse,
And pummeled her supple behind

The Limerick,
Restored

I set quite an ambitious goal
To give 90 girls my pole…
It resulted in pleasure
Far beyond measure,
But meanwhile, damaged my soul

I once knew a fella who tasted
A glob from each lady he basted…
Their vaginal boogers
Were sweeter than sugar,
With nary a drop ever wasted

He hated the urges that filled him,
And the battle of wills nearly killed him:
What a hideous curse
To constantly nurse
A lustful attraction to children

SECTION XII:
Sexual & Anatomical Obsessions

When I see girls spread em' and squat,
I get really horny—a lot
I hide and I watch
What ejects from your crotch;
Your pee is incredibly hot

SECTION XIII:
Other/Miscellaneous

The Limerick,
Restored

A svelte brunette vamp named Delphine
Is really feeling quite green:
A dong down her throat,
Her chin tickled by scrote,
She's repulsed by the size of the peen

After a pounding most loud,
'Twas a pungent post-coital cloud
Left limp and exhausted,
The dame's semen-frosted,
The gent assuredly proud

A loon had fanatical notions
Regarding his seminal potions:
Thought death was averted
Each time it was squirted,
Requiring gallons of lotion

A vegan gal made no exception
For her man's meaty erection:
For his one-eyed goat
Never entered her throat;
His cum was reserved for conception

A hooker who dabbled in stocks
Got tips while sucking the cocks...
Her big bets were winning
But she so loved her sinning,
She never stopped selling her box

A hotel-goer bedded the maidsy—
Seduced her, and rammed her like crazy...
After the fuck,
He tipped her a buck
And said, "Sorry, but I might be AIDSy."

The Limerick,
Restored

The bald, fleshy oyster of Maeve
Got wet when, once, in a cave
A snakey-snake slithered
And sent her atwitter,
Brushing her pussy unshaved

A young first-timer, inchoate,
Wasn't sure quite how to blow it…
So she gobbled it all,
Left her lover enthralled—
Complete with a cumshot to show it

When pilots fucked on the plane,
They'd earn some post-mortem fame…
Electrical glitches
From squirt on the switches
Caused them to fall like the rain

SECTION XIII:
Other/Miscellaneous

A young gal felt like running and hiding
From all of the hissing and chiding…
Some red stained her jeans
And the boys made a scene;
She'd shed her uterine lining

I'm surprised that a nerd from my school
Has Bimbofied, making me drool
I see she drools too,
But it's vaginal goo,
Her leg sopping wet from the grool

Going alone for a schvitz
Can sometimes be kinda the pits:
Over-talkative guys
Of generous size
With hairy and jiggling tits

The Limerick,
Restored

An athletic gall, name of Mallory,
Always counted her calories…
But she gained a few pounds
Worth of cum (almost drowned),
So great was her seminal salary

My lady is wild and loose,
With a labia huge like a moose,
I yank and I tug,
Just working those slugs,
For eruptions of sweet lady juice

I cooked up a pizza, al forno
That I ate with a hot side of porno:
My extra bologna,
So hard and bony,
Delivered a creamy DiGiorno

A fella's perfect-sized cock
Fit in like a key in a lock
So when he took a pill
To increase his fill,
It gave her a vaginal shock

There once was a fine deipnosophist
Debating a dinner philosophist
A sapiosexual,
The hot intellectual
Wondered if she could pulloffa tryst

In an act of grand histrionics,
She faked an orgasm, tectonic
Though not real, I'm flattered
So my goo, it still splattered
Hearing a moan so euphonic

The Limerick,
Restored

A man was left feeling lugubrious
After so many babes, pulchritudinous
Teased the poor guy
For his sad little fry;
Embarrassed by gals multitudinous

A shake, for extra nutrition
Was key to a lad's fitness mission
The blend was enhanced
With cream from his pants,
On orders from his physician

A skank once gave me a sign
That she'd let me get into her 'gine:
She was a deaf seller
Who signed "Come and get her."
I signed back, "That ass is divine."

She used a technique, epiplectic
To make me feel dyspeptic…
I said, "Inches of six
Is above-average dick,"
Winning out with my own dialectic

A nubile, clean and shampooed,
Felt that she wasn't quite through
But a second shower
Of germ on her flower
Left her plush and renewed

There once was a subnormal cretin
Wet-lipped from what he was eatin'…
Sure, he was dumb,
But with talented tongue,
His sexual prospects were sweetened

The Limerick,
Restored

A dude with a problem, genetic
Couldn't help but be rather frenetic:
He shook like a dog
When inserting his log,
For sex that was quite energetic

After being abused for his tic,
He became quite a nasty old prick:
He said with a stutter,
"I'll blast out my butter
If you s-s-s-s-suck my dick."

Patient, sweet, and avuncular
With a virgin whose balls were caruncular,
The dame drew a line
When she spotted some slime
Ooze from a boil, carbuncular

I maximize my exertion,
And can't keep up my act of perversion:
My load comes so fast,
That I cannot last,
Exhausting too close to insertion

I've heard that if you date a runner,
Her stride is what makes her a stunner:
She knows about rhythm,
To draw out your jism,
And makes you a very hard cummer

In spite of the size of his bone,
He was completely alone:
When it comes to big dongs,
Two feet is too long
To stuff into vaginal zones

The Limerick,
Restored

I once knew a hot teenage climber,
A perfect ten or a niner…
Turns out her belayer
Would very soon lay her,
Even though she was a minor

A sexpot, down at the tavern
Got me harder than any could fathom:
The way that she dripped
Really gave me the kicks
When she opened her wet little cavern

Over seafood, I noticed her garter…
Got so hot that I skipped all my starters
Went straight for dessert,
To give her a squirt
Of my pickly, masculine tartar

324

SECTION XIII:
Other/Miscellaneous

A penniless, pretty brunette
Had a plan to wipe out her debt:
Find the banker who loaned,
And chug on his bone,
And slurp up his white vinaigrette

The science of reproduction
Is simply a matter of suction:
The penis, a plunger,
Plunges down under,
Causing a spermy induction

A charmer I knew, on the trolley
Seduced a rider named Molly
On their ride to work,
She gave him a jerk,
Squirting his cum in a volley

The Limerick,
Restored

I fucked quite a hot engineer
And whispered hot math in her ear…
When it came to cumming,
I tickled her plumbing,
And worked all her angles and gears

After all of my cum was secreted,
My mojo was all but depleted:
My semen expired,
I was so tired,
From all of the gals I had seeded

For gals, peripheral vision
Is attuned with a mighty precision:
For creeps all abound
Licking chops like a hound;
Predators in their position

With my virile masculine vegetable,
I found a gal quite susceptible
She gobbled my carrot,
Performing with merit,
And finding it highly digestible

The problem with sex on the beach
Is the places the sand tends to reach:
A moonlit beach tumble
Means grit on the grundle,
The balls, the puss, and the peach

Onto my dick did she hoist—
O joy, 'twas time to rejoice!
Her curves were appealing,
Her tits were worth feeling,
Her kitty was supple and moist!

The Limerick,
Restored

I once ran the one-hundred dash
To sink my meat into a gash…
But my need to be quick
Was bad news for my dick—
After racing, I noticed the rash

The problem with woman on top
Is sometimes she'll jump and she'll hop
Bent near in half,
You will injure my shaft
If you slam it and hear something pop

There once was a flibbertigibbet
Stopped talking when she heard a ribbet
'Twas a frog up her ass,
So her gossip stopped fast;
To explain it, she just had to fib it

Shaking her tits as she danced
Was how she invited romance…
She did the cha-cha
On my cucaracha
When I got into her pants

I once knew a hot, diseased bitch
With a pungent vaginal ditch
I quite liked the smell,
But her crabs were still hell,
And caused an unbearable itch

I once fucked a feminine cleft
On a woman of notable heft…
And when I was sucked in
To her pussy's third chin,
I was left feeling bereft

The Limerick,
Restored

A tennis pro, out in the courts
Late night, after the sports,
Used them for serving
Pussy for perving,
Running a brothel of sorts

A hard-nippled, blonde little fizgig
Married a media bigwig,
But she left the jerk,
'Cause his dick didn't work,
And now I can use her to jizz big

If you dress up to standards exacting,
It leads to much more mate attracting…
Just pack up your goods,
And avoid getting wood,
Or it will become too distracting

I finally bedded my crush,
But then I came down with the thrush
I had so much fun,
But it yellowed my tongue,
Slurping her vaginal mush

She went to a hot chiropractor,
Flaunting her sexual factors…
Her spine was aligned
As he pummeled her 'gine,
Cracking her back as he jacked her

I once met a hot little cripple
Who limb-wise, had only a triple…
And though she was paretic,
I liked her aesthetic,
And wanted to suck on her nipple

The Limerick,
Restored

Without any hobbies or riches,
None sought the meat of my britches…
But since I won the lottery,
And got into pottery,
I enjoy limitless bitches

There once was a fellow named Patrick
Seduced by a gal, geriatric…
But her pussy hung limp
Like a deflated blimp,
Causing his break, psychiatric

Give my nut sack a squeeze,
And you'll get a squirt of my cheese…
But keep it out of your mouth,
And the hole that's down south,
Or you might catch my disease

A virus that I had detected
Would have to be promptly corrected:
A goo, thick and yellow,
Oozed out of my fellow,
Which critters had sadly infected

My desire for coitus soured
When an incident sapped my willpower:
Her pussy appeared
Indescribably weird;
A cactus instead of a flower

One day, my condom supply
Ran entirely dry:
When I knocked up my girl,
I fled 'cross the world,
To hide from the kid in Shanghai

The Limerick,
Restored

Presenting her meaty beef curtain,
Its appearance left me uncertain…
But I still achieved hardness,
So I fucked her regardless,
To give her a vaginal spurtin'

An object meant for flotation
Can be used for a fine masturbation
The inflatable plastic
Will feel fantastic,
Given a rhythmic gyration

In an act, both gross and unlawful,
A chef tampered with the falafel…
His cum was devoured,
And in under an hour,
Her stomach was feeling quite awful

For hygiene, it is a *must,*
For appeasing your prurient lust,
That you're fresh and clean
Inside of your jeans,
And wash off your penile crust

His passionate, tireless thrusting
Led to a seminal busting
Covered in goo,
The gal said "Adieu,"
For she found all the semen disgusting

The moment the orgasm hits,
My semen comes out in a spritz
If you cover her hoochie,
And give it a smoochie,
It pleases her sexual bits

The Limerick,
Restored

As she orgasmed louder and louder,
I was becoming a doubter:
Her jubilation
Was exaggeration,
But still caused a squirt of my chowder

We live in a decent society,
And must act with the utmost propriety...
That's why it's true,
When my boner pops through,
I feel a flood of anxiety

By abstaining, I shall preserve
My reproductive reserves...
When I finally spurt,
The volume of 'gurt
Will leave the receiver unnerved

A feculent, puss-squirting pimple
Appeared on her labial dimple...
She made an appointment,
They put on some ointment,
That's it—the cure was that simple

During a strange altercation,
A wife performed a castration...
In town, they all talked of
His voice, raised an octave,
After his humiliation

When he finally faced his accuser,
She said to her jailed abuser:
"You threatened and choked me,
But you never broke me,
And now you're a jailbird loser."

The Limerick,
Restored

My robust erectile reflex
Leaves me frequently sleepless:
It pokes in my ribs
When I lie in my crib;
'Tis the biggest of all of my secrets

To deliver a sexual thrill,
Proceed with patience and skill…
And when you're going south,
Begin with your mouth
Before you deliver your drill

She was young, so I was quite guarded,
But let loose when I saw she was carded…
Her driver's ID
Had good news for me:
I could legally fuck her retarded

In an oral sex situation,
Here's a trick for effective fellation:
Soften the lips
While you slurp on his bits,
And you'll cause a delightful sensation

She was paralyzed from the waist down,
But that bitch could still go to town—
What she lacked in gyration
She made up in fellation,
And titties so supple and round

My penis, a miniscule hose,
Is too small to accommodate blows:
She comes in for my cock,
But her access is blocked
By the tip of her sizeable nose

The Limerick,
Restored

I only have five or ten dollars,
And I live in embarrassing squalor…
But I told this one honey
I have lots of money—
She'll bang me if I am a baller

I once fucked this floozie, Amanda
I pounded her on the veranda
And before she left,
I left on her chest
A gooey and wet memoranda

I fell totally head over heels
For this beauty who gave me the feels
But I was dismayed
When I learned she was paid,
And found out that her love wasn't real

SECTION XIII:
Other/Miscellaneous

It's a great thing when girls are trashy,
Because then they don't care if you're dashing
You're ugly as shit?
It don't matter one bit!
They'll always be down for a mashing

When weather is frigid and icy,
I have ways of keeping things spicy:
From cock-tip to grundle,
I keep myself bundled
In mouths where I fit rather nicely

My penis, proud and ascended,
Had its dimensions extended
But the pump popped my schlong,
And now that it's gone,
My life of delights has been ended

The Limerick,
Restored

Have you ever dated a talker?
She'll turn you into a gawker...
She has nothing to say
And will jabber all day,
But at least you can stare at her knockers

Due to my blessings financial,
My love prospects are quite expansile...
The lonely old ways
Of my indigent days
Replaced by pussy substantial

After our passionate kiss,
I noticed something I'd missed:
Right on her lip,
An oozing green drip,
From an unfortunate cyst

No signs, at the time, were detected
That her little puss was infected…
I was desirous,
But she had a virus,
More dire than any expected

Bullies heaved scorn and derision
At the boy with the botched circumcision—
A medical blunder
Had torn it asunder,
From slippage during incision

This biker babe, name of Charlee
Could perform a few feats rather gnarly
She'd be going to town,
Suckin' cock upside-down,
Balanced on top of her Harley

The Limerick,
Restored

My girl, a cyclist biker,
Loves when a stranger will spike her…
Let's meet by my Schwinn,
Then you stick it in,
And fuck her all day if you like her

I'm an athlete from excellent stock,
A square jaw and a powerful cock
And I'm ready to pound
Any gal in this town
Who's craving the thrust of a jock

We met in the copse for a slam,
But the pricklers were scratching the ma'am
In the thicket all bloody,
Dirty and muddy,
We opted to bag it, and scram

344

I excel in both looks and athletics,
For I'm blessed with some nifty genetics
My cock is a beaut
When I thrust in your chute;
A display of arousing kinetics

When young, pretty mothers are struggling,
Their measures, sometimes, are troubling
But when you've got the skills,
And dick pays the bills,
Tummies no longer are rumbling

Didn't know that she had a disorder,
But found out that my date was a hoarder…
With obsessions neurotic,
And delusions psychotic,
I'm sorry as hell that I gored her

The Limerick,
Restored

A waterbed moves like the ocean,
In sultry and sexual motion…
Just hop on the top,
Give your body a rock,
And hump 'till you fire your potion

I was gonna be fucking an elder…
'Twas going quite well, 'till I smelled her
So here is the moral:
I settled for oral,
And happily groaned as I gelled her

In sexing, to be the best,
You must receive adequate rest…
After fucking like crazy,
I'm fresh as a daisy,
Leaving my lovers impressed

When the baker cried out, "Please baste me!",
Her thirst made me feel quite hasty...
So like any guy should,
I basted her good,
Filling her hot little pastry

At a fancy, upper-class luncheon,
I revealed my seminal truncheon...
The ladies were shocked
By the sight of my cock,
And the men, to defend them, came punchin'

A nubile, young and pristine,
Attracts many when she turns eighteen...
But her lack of skills show
She has much room to grow,
For she is still sexually green

The Limerick,
Restored

I'll recommend something new:
Being fucked while you've got the flu
Use your mucus as lube
While he pummels your tube—
You'll feel refreshed from the screw

It is incredibly humbling,
When into a spiral you're stumbling,
To sell your own dick
For a dime or a nick,
And stop the damn stomach from rumbling

This hot little cougar, a fox,
Lures you in with her sexual talk
Once you're in her home,
Commence with the bone,
And cream in her sensual box

After getting a dance from a stripper,
I told her that I couldn't tip her…
So she pulled out my guy,
Yanked up on the fly,
And clenched my poor dick in the zipper

To properly take lots of fat dicks,
You need to receive lots of practice:
Instead of a weenie,
Use a zucchini,
But never a shovel or cactus

It is a serious question,
During a sucky-suck session:
"After chugging the flood
From my vascular spud,
Do you get bad indigestion?"

The Limerick,
Restored

For you, the position ideal
Is in front of my penis, and kneeled
Then get ready to eat
A serving of meat,
And swallow my slippery eel

A glistening field of wheat
I'll harvest tonight for a treat:
One whip of my scythe, and
She'll moan and she'll writhe,
Plowed by my glorious meat

I decided to try going keto,
So I would look good in a speedo
The problem, however,
Is my little lever
Is only the size of a frito

SECTION XIII:
Other/Miscellaneous

When a girl is being a flirt,
She'll get just as dirty as dirt…
So flirt right back at her,
What you say doesn't matter—
She'll let you get under her skirt

It's simply a matter of fact
That I have a particular knack
For making her cream
While she is reamed,
A talent that other men lack

Covered in my nasty bust,
The little prude was nonplussed:
She knew not what to say
As I blew her away,
Raising her hands in disgust

The Limerick,
Restored

My love has left me, and gone,
And the sadness is something I dwell on:
I can't stand my hiraeth
For this far-away life,
And the sweet pussy I used to gel on

I stuffed my cum-shooting giblet
Into her little pink piglet...
But I was so tired
From loads I had fired,
That I only squirted a driblet

My gal was a dirty two-timer,
So I dumped her and gave her a shiner
Now she is free,
So a hoe she will be;
A prolific and passionate slimer

Because I am sexually fearless,
I just had an STI near-miss…
Not that I'm a critic,
But a bitch syphilitic
Led to an itch rather cheerless

I picked up a hot little mami
Who I folded like origami
She was so flexible,
It made her quite sex-able,
Perfect to stuff with salami

Lately you haven't been mowing,
And all of your pubies are showing…
They've gotten so thick
That you can't see your dick,
And still they're continually growing

The Limerick,
Restored

At the beach with the tart, Maya Sweeney,
I noticed her sexy bikini…
It looked even more grand
Tossed onto the sand,
While Maya sucked on my weenie

My God, isn't life grand,
In the sun with our toes in the sand?
And a chick from Encino,
Wasted on vino,
Stroking my dick in her hand?

Soon as I let down my guard,
I fall madly in love very hard
If you don't love me back,
I'll sit down and whack
Until my poor penis is scarred

There once was a dashing alumnus,
Who they said had a member humongous
At the ten-year soirée,
I lent him a lay,
But then caught a penile fungus

I'm dapper and debonair,
And I catch her lascivious stare…
Once we're alone,
And we finally bone,
The tension will break in the air

When she was infected with yeast,
Our fucking quite suddenly ceased…
It was such a bummer
'Cause I couldn't plumb her,
Or pleasure her vaginal crease

The Limerick,
Restored

When you are wealthy and prosperous,
Their pussies burn hotter than phosphorous
But when you are poor,
They're cold as the floor—
Money's what gets em' hot for us

Her vag was so massive and gaping,
She did not even feel me raping…
Her big, baggy droop hole
Turns out, is a loophole
So rape charges I am escaping

In a derelict old athenaeum,
She licked on my sweet perineum
I'll come back with some buddies
To continue our studies…
The librarian's eager to see em'

A real slick player named Bart
Could hook up with any old tart…
He'd mess with their heads
To get em' in bed,
And then he would promptly depart

When I'm out with my dog on a walk,
All of the neighbors will gawk:
While out on our stroll,
We're thinking of hole,
Which hardens up both of our cocks

Beneath buzzing neon glow,
A hooker robotically blows…
She dreams of a chance
To make it in dance,
But this is the life that she chose

The Limerick,
Restored

Though my penis is stalwart and trusty,
My skills are a little bit rusty...
But with foreplay and luck
I'll impress when I fuck,
As long as I'm lovingly lusty

She straddled me in the river,
And my cock was the thing that I'd give her...
All my whitewater
Shot up in her otter,
As semen was promptly delivered

Not to brag, but I have to confess,
My cock has one hell of a flex:
After the boff,
It doesn't go soft,
Unlike all of the rest

A vegan was instantly shunned
When they learned she had been drinking cum:
She broke vegan code
By chugging the loads
From out of a penile gun

He went in raw, like a moron,
So his penis he now has a sore on…
Didn't even catch names,
So now he's ashamed,
And just wants his horrible sore gone

A cheese-making hipster named Marty
Fucked a cheese-loving gal at a party…
The cheese-loving nerd
Delivered his curd:
A hot liquid stream of Havarti

The Limerick,
Restored

At a funny farm for trainable nitwits,
Full of droolers having seizures and shit-fits,
I fucked one with ease
But I have a disease,
And I'm hoping I didn't transmit it

The tool I use for the peein'
Is hulky and herculean…
It rises with veins,
Leaving pussies in pain—
After we fuck, they are fleein'

I can't help but recoil and cuss
When I see a cunt leaking pus…
When they are infected,
I'm badly affected,
But I am a bit of a wuss

My technique, when I am on top,
Is simply to writhe and to flop...
For me it is great,
But less for my date,
Who usually tells me to stop

When I am out on my hustle,
Seeking some cash for a tussle,
I find lonely souls
To stuff all their holes,
Using my penile muscle

I'm a habitué of the brothel,
But I think fornication is awful...
They don't see my cock
'Cause I just want to talk:
I'm lonely, but I am lawful

The Limerick,
Restored

A tight-bodied, nubile teaser
Met her match in a geezer:
She went in with her hand,
But his tiny gland
Could only be milked with a tweezer

OTHER WORKS BY
THE POXY BROTHERS

Save for this book, all of the Poxy Brothers' works are stashed away in the Family Archives. However, the following represents a brief selection of their proudest literary accomplishments:

The Nudgelkludge

The Sequel 3, Part I: A Biannual Trilogy Told in Seven Thrilling Installments

Blastoff: A Brief History of the Space Hoax

Moist Libations: An Uncle Remus™ Mystery

The Taxidermied Infant

Boys in Bloom: Walking Your Boys Through Puberty (A Guide for Uncles)

Made in the USA
Middletown, DE
20 July 2023